THE WISTERIA BUSH

A Play In Two Acts

By
Jo Vander Voort

SAMUEL FRENCH, INC.

45 WEST 25TH STREET   NEW YORK 10010
7623 SUNSET BOULEVARD HOLLYWOOD 90046
LONDON   TORONTO

Copyright ©, 1980, 1987, by Jo Vander Voort

ALL RIGHTS RESERVED

IMPORTANT BILLING AND CREDIT REQUIREMENTS

All producers of THE WISTERIA BUSH *must* give credit to the Author of the Play in all programs distributed in connection with performances of the Play and in all instances in which the title of the Play appears for purposes of advertising, publicizing or otherwise exploiting the Play and/or a production. The name of the Author *must* also appear on a separate line, in which no other name appears, immediately following the title, and *must* appear in size of type not less than fifty percent the size of the title type.

the wisteria bush

by Jo Vander Voort

Winner of the 1981 Circle Players-Gannett Foundation nation-wide original play competition

May 30, 1981

Premiere Performance	2 p.m.
Circle Benefit Performance	8 p.m.

Directed by Paul R. Klapper   **Produced by Jan Belcher**

Set Designed by Fred Schlatter   **Lighting Designed by Steve Loftin**

Cast

Ruthie Ann Castro . . . . Mauna Faye Midgett
Mama Wallace . . . . Barbara Jones
Acia Darling . . . . Becky Coutras
Miss Elly . . . . Ruthmary Cobb
Sybil Parker . . . . Jan Meredith

CHARACTERS

(in order of appearance)

RUTHIE ANN CASTRO — *A woman in her late 30's, early 40's. She's rather plain looking, not by nature, but rather by choice. She lives with her mother.*

MAMA WALLACE — *Ruthie Ann's mother. In her late 50's, 60's. A country woman, who has lived in the same house, most of her life.*

ACIA DARLING — *An attractive woman, the same age as Ruthie Ann. Her husband is mayor of the town and she and Ruthie Ann have known each other all their lives. They are best friends.*

MISS ELLY — *Mama's best friend and next door neighbor. She is about the same age as Mama.*

SYBIL PARKER — *A fat woman in her late 30's, early 40's. Ruthie Ann and Acia's friend. She's a school teacher.*

THE PLACE

Coleridge, Alabama

THE SETTING

Living, dining room of Mama Wallace

THE TIME

1975

ACT ONE

Late afternoon in April

ACT TWO

Scene One
The next morning

Scene Two
That night

THE WISTERIA BUSH

ACT ONE

*Setting: The living, dining room of MAMA WALLACE. The fur-
nishings are worn, but comfortable. An over-stuffed sofa and
matching chair, end tables with mis-matched lamps and a
free-standing bookcase. There are crocheted doilies every-
where in every color. The coffee table is crowded with family
pictures in frames and there's a dining table, chairs and a
side-board to one side of the room. The table is covered with
an oilcloth tablecloth. The over all effect of the room is like
walking back in history 50 years.*

*As the lights come up, RUTHIE ANN is setting the table
with three napkins, coffee cups and in the center of the table,
has placed a bowl full of chocolate chip cookies. She is dressed
in a pair of dark slacks and a drab-colored blouse.*

RUTHIE ANN. I swear Mama, I don't know why ya don't
buy ya some decent dishes. *(She holds up one of the cups to the
light and makes a very disapproving face.)* These ole cups came
outta Quaker Oats boxes, 25 years ago.

*(Enter MAMA WALLACE, she's dressed in a faded gingham
housedress and is wearing her hair in a knot at the back of her head.
She has on glasses and a pair of old shoes with socks, with the tops
rolled down. Her overall demeanor is one of quaintness.)*

MAMA. *(upon entering)* Never ask you and your friends to meet here anyways. *(She goes to the table and abruptly begins to remove the dishes.)*

RUTHIE ANN. *(goes to her mother)* I got that all arranged and look what...

MAMA. If my dishes ain't good enough for ya ... drink outtava mason jar for all I care.

RUTHIE ANN. All right!

MAMA. Fool girl, these dishes are priceless antiques.

RUTHIE ANN. *(sarcastic)* I apologize for insultin your antiques.

MAMA. *(stops removing the dishes and RUTHIE ANN begins to re-arrange them on the table)* If ya wanted fancier dishes, why didn't ya unpack some of your own? They been sittin out in the garage in boxes now for a year.

RUTHIE ANN. I'm gonna be leavin here anytime now, and wouldn't it be real silly to go to all the trouble to unpack my things and then just have to put 'um away again.

MAMA. *(Not impressed. She's heard this story before.)* Girl, you been sayin ya gonna be leavin for a year ... *you're still here.*

RUTHIE ANN. Just a mix-up, that's all it is. Soon as Harry comes around to his senses, he'll send for me. *(pause)* See if the coffee's through perkin, will ya.

MAMA. *(staring at her)* I'll look at it for ya, Ruthie Ann, *(as she exits to the kitchen)* but next time you have a get together here, unpack some of ya own things, ya hear me? *(She exits to the kitchen.)*

RUTHIE ANN. *(shouting at her)* I hear ya! *(The telephone rings and RUTHIE ANN picks it up.)* Hello. *(pause)* No, not yet...expect her anytime now. *(pause)* Yeah, ya at the courthouse or where? *(pause)* Fine, I'll tell her. *(She hangs up the phone.)*

(Enter MAMA from the kitchen.)

MAMA. Who was that?

RUTHIE ANN. Milton checkin up on Acia. *(pause)* How's the coffee?

MAMA. Coffee?

RUTHIE ANN. *(exasperated)* Ya went to check on the coffee.

MAMA. *(as though it's not important)* Forgot to look... heard the phone...

RUTHIE ANN. *(starts to exit to the kitchen)* I have to do everthing around here.

MAMA. Is that a fact. This is the first day ya been up before the dinner hour in a week...wouldn't be up yet, wasn't for this here meetin.

RUTHIE ANN. I do my share! All the laundry...

MAMA. Those huge mounds of dirty laundry are *yours.* Fore you moved back, I had one wash rag and a towel a week to wash. *(pause)* Never seen anybody use so many towels and wash rags in all my life.

RUTHIE ANN. *(as she exits to the kitchen)* Sorry it bothers ya that I'm a clean person. *(She exits.)*

MAMA. *(Goes to the bookcase and picks up a gardening book. She brings it back to her easy chair and sits down and begins to read the book. To herself.)* That's really somethin. *(hollers out to RUTHIE ANN)* Ruthie Ann, you know ya can shock a wisteria bush into bloomin, by hittin it with a shovel?

RUTHIE ANN. *(Comes back into the room and is carrying a sugar bowl and creamer. She walks to the table and sets them both down.)* Where's the saccharin? Sybil's on a diet and can't be drinkin sugar in her coffee.

MAMA. Been on a diet for 20 years...she's still fat. *(pause)* Got that wisteria out by the front gate's never bloomed. Thought cause of that ole oak, wasn't gettin enough sun...just needs to be shocked, that's all.

RUTHIE ANN. What are you talkin about?

MAMA. *(Gets up with the book and goes over to RUTHIE ANN.)* Look here! This here bush is just bloomin up a storm and it's all because it was hit real hard with a shovel.

RUTHIE ANN. That's a bunch a nonsense. *(as she takes the book and looks at it)* People that wrote this here book, drove around till they found a bush bloomin like this. They've said all this stuff, just to *sell* this book.

MAMA. *(grabs the book back from her)* You gettin awful high and mighty, bout somethin ya know nothin about.

RUTHIE ANN. You never give me credit for knowin nothin. *(pause)* Gardenin' happened to be Harry's hobby...never hit a bush to make it bloom either. We had the prettiest yard in Coleridge. Why his roses were the talk of the neighborhood.

MAMA. *(Disgusted, returns to her chair and flops down with the gardening book.)* Don't know about his roses, but he was the talk of the whole town!

RUTHIE ANN. Don't you get started on him...

MAMA. The day he took off with that other woman, we all said...

RUTHIE ANN. *(mad)* I don't give a damn what ya'll said!

MAMA. You're the one brought up Harry's name.

RUTHIE ANN. I was talkin about his roses, that's all. *(pause)* Anway, he was mesmerized by that person. She was a *witch*. Why everbody knew she was a witch. She worked some kinda black spell on him. Soon as he gets outta that spell, he'll come runnin back to me.

MAMA. You're wastin your time moonin over somebody, who ain't never gonna come back.

RUTHIE ANN. He'll be back, ya just wait and see. *(pause)* All our stuff is out there in the garage. Twenty years of marriage is packed away out there in boxes. No man is gonna walk off and forget 20 years. All his shirts... ties...bowlin trophies. Harry misses those things alot and when his wanderlust is outta his system, believe you me, I'll see him again. *(pause)* That's why I don't wantta unpack those things...those are Harry's things.

MAMA. Figure if a man runs off and leaves his wife and things, ya gotta right to take what's his and make it yours.

RUTHIE ANN. That's just plain stupid, Mama. Now what am I gonna do with a bunch of ole bowlin trophies. *(pause)* I'm not talkin about this anymore...I gotta splittin headache...gotta get me a aspirin. *(She starts to exit to the bedroom.)*

MAMA. *(concerned)* You oughta see a doctor bout them headaches you been havin. It ain't natural to have that many headaches.

RUTHIE ANN. Tension! Tension is what causes my headaches.

MAMA. For the life of me, I don't know what ya gotta be tense about. Gotta roof over your head...plenty to eat...don't work, cause your Mama's supportin ya.

RUTHIE ANN. That's it right there. You're always throwin up that you're supportin me.

MAMA. Well I am!

RUTHIE ANN. But what am I suppose to do?

MAMA. Would help a might, if you was to consider findin yourself a job.

RUTHIE ANN. There's no work to he had in Coleridge Alabama. There's just nothin here in this small town's not taken.

MAMA. I know for a fact Milton's lookin for somebody out at his place. Acia told me so.

RUTHIE ANN. Do you really expect me to work in a beer joint?

MAMA. Blue Moon Cafe ain't strictly a beer joint... serve food and all. You could pick up some big tips out there and...

RUTHIE ANN. You don't know what you're talkin about, why Harry told me...

MAMA. Don't wantta hear what Harry said...hung out there enough himself. *(pause)* Ain't that where he met his floozy?

RUTHIE ANN. *(angry with her mother)* You are makin my head feel like it's gettin ready to bust. *(She exits to the bedroom.)*

MAMA. *(starts to go to the kitchen)* Harry, Harry, Harry's all I hear around here. *(hollers out to RUTHIE ANN)* Ain't nothin wrong with workin at The Blue Moon...work is work. Don't mean ya gotta go along with nothin ya don't like.

(There's a knock at the door.)

MAMA. I'm comin.

(another knock)

MAMA. I said I'm comin...hold your horses.

(She opens the door and enter ACIA DARLING. ACIA is wearing very tight fitting blue jeans and a tight fitting tee shirt. Her hair is long and she's wearing it loose and flowing. She's a very sexy woman, but not in a vulgar way. She wears her sexiness like some women wear a new hat to church. She knows it's very becoming, but she doesn't flaunt it.)

ACIA. *(upon entering)* Thank God, it's some cooler in here. *(She begins to fan herself with a handkerchief she's carrying.)* Boy is it hot out there and this here is just April. Woulda worn me some short shorts today, but Milton woulda thrown a fit.

MAMA. Is hot for April...come May we're all gonna be dyin.

ACIA. I think we should hold this here reunion in the fall, but Milton says what with football and all, nobody would pay it much mind.

MAMA. Acia, did your wisteria by the front porch bloom last year?

ACIA. Don't recall if it bloomed or not. Remember Milton cuttin it back though. *(as she looks around the room)*

Where's Ruthie Ann?

MAMA. In there takin an aspirin.

ACIA. She got another one of her migraine head-aches?

MAMA. *(shakes her head yes)* And she needs to go see a doctor. Would you talk to her...I think she'd listen to you.

ACIA. Those headaches are all in her head.

MAMA. I know they're in her head and they're beginnin to worry the fire outta me.

ACIA. *(laughs)* What I mean Mama Wallace is. *(She touches her fingers to her head near the temple.)*

MAMA. You sayin Ruthie Ann's crackin up?

ACIA. I'm sayin...she's lettin her emotions rule her head and it's causin...

MAMA. *(interrupts)* Who named you the doctor around here. Ya been to medical school?

ACIA. Not yet, but if I had a mind to...

MAMA. Then you got no business diagnosen some-thin.

ACIA. *(shrugs her shoulders)* Sybil's not here yet, huh?

MAMA. *(shakes her head no)* And she's on another one of her diets. Gotta go find her some saccharin. *(as she exits to the kitchen)* By the way, Milton called ya.

ACIA. What the hell did he want?

MAMA. *(grins at her)* Ruthie Ann said he's checkin up on ya.

ACIA. I can't get outta that man's sight, he don't start to pester me. Next fellow I marry's gonna be barely outta diapers...too young to know if I'm comin or goin. *(She goes to the phone and picks it up.)* Where was Milton?

MAMA. Don't know. *(hollers out to RUTHIE ANN)* Ruthie Ann, Acia's here. Where was Milton when he called?

(RUTHIE ANN comes back into the room and is mopping her head with a wash cloth.)

RUTHIE ANN. What'd ya say Mama? *(See ACIA and goes over and gives her a big hug.)* Glad ya got here. *(stands back and looks at her)* Crime to look so sexy in a plain tee shirt. If I put on a shirt like that, I'd look like a pregnant heifer.

ACIA. *(laughs)* Ya would not either. *(pause)* Where was Milton when he called?

RUTHIE ANN. Told me he was at...

MAMA. *(to RUTHIE ANN)* There you go, messin up another wash rag.

RUTHIE ANN. *(to MAMA)* Feels good on my head... besides I do the laundry. *(to ACIA)* He's at the courthouse. *(ACIA begins to dial the phone.)*

RUTHIE ANN. *(to MAMA)* Would ya mind bringin in the coffee? Sybil should be here any minute. *(MAMA starts to exit.)* And don't forget the saccharin.

ACIA. *(into the phone)* Gertrude, this is Acia Darlin...is he there? *(pause)* Well, let me talk to him.

MAMA. *(to RUTHIE ANN)* There's no point for somebody that fat to drink saccharin in their coffee. *(She exits to the kitchen.)*

ACIA. *(to RUTHIE ANN)* Sounds like Gertrude's gotta cold.

RUTHIE ANN. From walkin around with her nose so high in the air. One'd think she was head of communications at the Pentagon. *(She walks to the kitchen door and swings it open, and to her mother.)* It'd make Sybil happy to have saccharin in her coffee, ok?

ACIA. *(into the phone)* Milton, ya called me.

MAMA. *(swings the door open and to RUTHIE ANN)* Not gonna help her one single bit. *(She closes the door.)*

ACIA. *(to MILTON)* I could give a rat's ass about her family history. *(pause)* Well, you're not exactly runnin the Copa Cabanna out there. *(pause)* Look at it like this...ya need a waitress. So it should bring in alotta business for ya, if she's screwed ever guy in Freestone County. *(pause)* It is funny. Can't this wait till I get home? *(pause)* Lord yes Milton, I'll come directly home. Why I won't even pat a little dog on the way. *(She slams down the phone and to RUTHIE ANN.)* I can't take a pee, that he don't ask me what I'm fixin' to do.

RUTHIE ANN. He loves ya.

ACIA. *(gets her purse and takes out a cigarette)* Where's a ashtray? You hide'um again?

RUTHIE ANN. *(Goes to where she's hidden the ashtray, behind some books in the bookcase.)* Puffin on cancer sticks gonna stunt your growth.

ACIA. *(sticks out her rather ample chest)* Hadn't so far. *(pause)* It's not love when a man is so jealous, he makes life miserable for ya. Why, I can't even look at the paper boy Milton don't think I'm gettin ready to lay him.

RUTHIE ANN. You're exaggeratin. *(pause)* Besides, that Reynolds boy's ugly as a mud fence. Gotta face only a mother or Baptist preacher could love. *(Pause. They both laugh.)* How I wish Harry'd been jealous of me.

ACIA. *(Sits down in the easy chair and shakes off her shoes and leans her head back and tries to blow smoke rings in the air. After a moment's hesitation.)* You don't know how lucky you are Harry ran off with another woman. *(as she reflects a moment)* Wish Milton would run off with another woman. *(pause)* Hell, I wouldn't care if he ran off with another man, just so he ran off.

RUTHIE ANN. You oughta be ashamed talkin like that.

(MAMA enters from the kitchen.)

MAMA. Brought the coffee...couldn't find the saccharin. *(She goes to the table and sets the coffee down.)*

RUTHIE ANN. You're bein stubborn and not lookin for it. You see no point to it and therefore, you're puttin your will on somebody else.

MAMA. I'm puttin nothin on nobody. We don't have any saccharin!

RUTHIE ANN. *(leaves the room mad)* Yes we do!

MAMA. Lord, that girl gets more cantankerous ever day. *(pause)* I was over in Athens last Wednesday evenin.

ACIA. Is that a fact? *(She walks to where the gardening book is and begins to thumb through it.)* See ya got yourself a new book.

MAMA. Got some interestin things in it too. *(pause)* Speakin of interestin things...saw somebody looked like you in Athens on Wednesday. *(Getting no response from ACIA who continues to look at the book.)* Course, guess it wasn't though, cause this girl was with a man didn't look a thing like Milton.

ACIA. *(referring to the book)* Pretty pictures in here. *(pause)*

Suppose there's lots of girls look like me Mama Wallace. After all, I'm just a average lookin girl.

MAMA. *(eyes her)* Wouldn't say that. Not too many forty year old women, wear their hair long and flowin down their back. *(pause)* Makes ya *very* distinguishable.

ACIA. *(Acting as though she is bored with the whole conversation.)* I do wear my hair *up* once in awhile.

MAMA. Wear it up last Wednesday?

ACIA. *(still bored)* Can't recall...could have. Has been awful hot lately. *(pause)* Where'd you get this book?

MAMA. Was a present from a friend.

ACIA. Must be from Miss Elly...considerin she's the only friend you got.

(MAMA glares at her and RUTHIE ANN comes back into the room and is waving the bottle of saccharin in the air.)

RUTHIE ANN. *(sarcastically)* *This* is saccharin...was right next to the vitamins.

MAMA. Didn't see it.

RUTHIE ANN. Sure you didn't.

ACIA. *(Going to have some fun at RUTHIE ANN'S expense.)* You know your Mama saw somebody who looked just like me in Athens last Wednesday...would ya believe it. Course, the man she was with, didn't look nothin like Milton.

RUTHIE ANN. *(Becomes flustered. ACIA enjoys her discomfort and MAMA just glares at ACIA.)* Ah...well, it was surely a mistake. *(pause)* Mama, you wasn't even in Athens on Wednesday.

MAMA. Was too. Me and Miss Elly went to the five and

dime. Got some material for a dress I'm gonna make for the Homecomin. *(pause)* She helped me pick out the pattern.

ACIA. *(delivered with insinuation)* You and Miss Elly sure are *good* friends.

MAMA. None better. Why we been best friends all our lives...when our husbands died...

ACIA. *Odd,* neither of ya got married again.

MAMA. Why should we get married again. We was able to take care of ourselves.

ACIA. Seems kinda funny that's all. Two ladies runnin around together all the time. *(pause)* Guess I never saw either of ya with a man.

MAMA. Ain't nothin funny about it at all...we did so see men.

RUTHIE ANN. Acia, Mama had some dates, but she didn't have much choice in this town. It's not like we're livin in Birmingham, where the pickins are plentiful.

ACIA. Been a few eligible men around here. *(Deciding to drop the whole conversation and to RUTHIE ANN.)* What's this here committee suppose to do?

RUTHIE ANN. Pick a Homecomin Queen...we need to get...

MAMA. *(as she exits to the bedroom)* Men around this town was flat-out addle brained. I'm gonna get my material and show ya that I was too over in Athens. *(She exits.)*

RUTHIE ANN. *(to ACIA softly)* Did you see Mama in Athens on Wednesday?

ACIA. Sure didn't...but she evidently saw me.

RUTHIE ANN. Acia, you better be more careful. Milton catches you runnin around on him, he'll kill ya.

ACIA. He's not about to kill nobody. *(pause)* Less he *bores'um* to death.

RUTHIE ANN. Just the same...if Mama saw ya, somebody else might.

ACIA. So what. Nothin but a bunch of hicks around here anyways. Let'um get a eyeful. *(She goes and picks up the bowl of cookies.)* This all we're gonna have to eat on?

RUTHIE ANN. Sybil's watchin her weight.

ACIA. In the wrong direction. *(pause)* She's gotta sickness eatin like that and oughta see a psychiatrist. Why no man in his right head's gonna pay any mind to a tub of lard.

RUTHIE ANN. Shouldn't talk about Sybil like that.

ACIA. She knows she's a tub of lard. She's liable to wind up in a early grave, if I don't keep remindin her.

RUTHIE ANN. *(completely out of the blue)* Harry ran off with a fat lady...I was told. *(ACIA looks at her like, oh no, here we go again.)* He was mesmerized, ya know.

ACIA. *(bored)* Yeah, I know...you've told me a hundred times.

RUTHIE ANN. Well, he was. If Milton hada fired that woman...

ACIA. He had no reason to fire her. She didn't do nothin wrong.

RUTHIE ANN. She stole my husband. A bar maid at The Blue Moon Cafe. *(pause)* All the vice in this county comes outta that joint ya'll own.

ACIA. *(This makes her mad.)* You never even been out there, Ruthie Ann Castro. You don't know what the hell you're talkin about.

RUTHIE ANN. Why I've heard...

ACIA. Grow up! You act like you're livin in the nineteenth century. Milton runs a respectable place out there and now that he's mayor too, he can keep an eye...

RUTHIE ANN. You probably didn't even vote for him.

ACIA. *(ignores this)* Milton felt like it was his civic duty to run for office. *(pause)* He may be a borin jealous husband, but he's a true patriot.

RUTHIE ANN. Rollin in vice and squalor.

ACIA. *(This makes her even madder.)* Well, he and me are keepin ourselves busy. *(pause)* Look at you! You're just shrivelin up like a ole maid...sittin around moanin and groanin over Harry...gettin your stupid migraine headaches and lovin ever minute of your malady.

RUTHIE ANN. At least I'm not makin a fool of myself by runnin around with anything in pants.

ACIA. *(Goes over to her purse and takes out another cigarette.)* More than one way to make a fool of yourself. What I'm doin makes me happy...are you?

(MAMA enters from the bedroom and is carrying a piece of pink cotton material and a dress pattern.)

MAMA. Here's my material. *(Holds out the material toward ACIA, as though this does prove she was in Athens on Wednesday.)* And this is the pattern Miss Elly helped me pick out. *(She shoves the pattern right under ACIA'S nose.)*

ACIA. But Mama Wallace, this here pattern has ruffles around the neck.

MAMA. *(forgets the prior incident)* Miss Elly thinks they

might be real flatterin.

ACIA. No way...it's just too babyfied for ya. Ain't it, Ruthie Ann. *(holds the pattern out to her)*

RUTHIE ANN. *(still mad at ACIA)* Havin a malady which effects my brain...I'm hardly one to ask such an important question to.

ACIA. *(ignores her and to MAMA)* Try a gathered neckline. Be more becomin on ya.

MAMA. Why didn't I think of that? My good pearls would go perfect with a gathered neckline.

ACIA. *(to RUTHIE ANN)* You done any work at all, on this Homecomin thing?

RUTHIE ANN. Another important question to a brain defective person.

MAMA. *(to RUTHIE ANN)* What is this brain defect you keep talkin about?

RUTHIE ANN. My migraine headaches. You and Acia think I bring'um on myself, don't ya. *(They neither one answer.)* A act of God...they are a flat-out act of God.

ACIA. We need to get to the business at hand here. I didn't come here to talk about acts of God. Now, have you done anything at all on this Homecomin business?

RUTHIE ANN. Sent out the nomination forms.

ACIA. Is that it?

RUTHIE ANN. I got some back.

ACIA. Where the hell are they?

RUTHIE ANN. *(Goes to the bookcase and gets the forms and MAMA goes to her chair and begins to take apart the pattern and look at it.)* A piddly response...we got a piddly response. *(pause)* We're gonna have to pick our queen from these girls, cause we might not hear from anybody else.

ACIA. Let's get to it. Milton's liable to be callin back anytime now.

RUTHIE ANN. We have to wait. Sybil's on this here committee too.

ACIA. Damn it, she knew the time she was suppose to be here. *(pause)* I'll wait a little bit longer, if ya get me somethin stronger to drink than coffee.

RUTHIE ANN. We are havin coffee!

MAMA. *(to ACIA)* Bottle of wine in the bottom cupboard under the sink.

RUTHIE ANN. Mama, you shouldn't have liquor in this house.

MAMA. It's my house, I'll have what I want. *(to ACIA)* Go get it and bring *two* glasses.

ACIA. Sure enough. *(She exits to the kitchen.)*

RUTHIE ANN. *(disgusted)* If ya'll drink liquor, I just made this here coffee for nothin.

MAMA. You and Sybil can drink it.

RUTHIE ANN. I don't even like coffee that much and Sybil says the caffeine makes her nervous.

MAMA. Caffeine baloney! It's all that starchy food.

RUTHIE ANN. *(getting annoyed)* You don't believe she's tryin to lose weight, so you're gonna set there and judge her. You gonna hang onto what you think, no matter what.

MAMA. When she loses her fat, I'll change my mind.

RUTHIE ANN. I'm gonna pray she gets skinny as a rail, just to show you up.

MAMA. It'd take a whole church prayin to get her skinny.

RUTHIE ANN. Where is she anyway? School was out thirty minutes ago.

MAMA. Probably kept somebody after class.

RUTHIE ANN. Never! You know she hates school.

MAMA. Don't know why she became a school teacher then. When ya teach school, you gotta be figurin on spendin a good deal of your time there.

RUTHIE ANN. Her Mama pushed her into bein a school teacher. *(pause)* Sybil wanted to be a ballet dancer.

MAMA. *(laughs)* She'd a lost some fat doin that, cause she woulda starved to death.

RUTHIE ANN. *(mad)* For all you know, she might have become a famous dancer. Why she might even be on Broadway, by now.

MAMA. When cows fly!

(Enter ACIA carrying two glasses and a bottle of wine. She goes over to where MAMA is sitting and puts it all down. She uncaps the wine and pours them a drink.)

ACIA. This should put hair on our chest.

MAMA. Never wanted no hair on my chest. Was always some concerned about the hair on my upper lip. *(points to her lip)* See, I gotta faint mustache.

RUTHIE ANN. Mama, you don't have any mustache.

MAMA. Do so, and it don't seem right for a woman to have one either.

ACIA. *(takes a closer look)* Can hardly see it really. If it bothers ya, why don't ya get some kinda remover?

MAMA. Never heard of such a thing.

ACIA. Well, Old Man Black don't carry nothin that

sophisticated down at his hick store, but next time I'm in Athens, I'll pick ya up some.

MAMA. Thank ya Acia. Thought I was gonna have to start shavin in my ole age. You saved me some worry about it. *(pause)* This wine really hits the spot on a hot day like this. *(pause)* Me and Miss Elly have always enjoyed our wine. Even when it was taboo for women to drink, we'd slip around and do it anyway.

ACIA. It's good and that's a fact. Ruthie Ann, come on and have some...might help your malady.

RUTHIE ANN. *(very sanctimonious)* Drinkin's a real sin...caused more homes to be destroyed. Little children without their Daddy's, all because of drinkin. It's a disgrace, is what it is.

ACIA. Bull! Boredom destroys homes. Plain out and out boredom.

RUTHIE ANN. Just you wait. One of these days, when Milton runs off with one of those drunken floozies at The Blue Moon, you'll see what I mean.

ACIA. Milton ain't gonna run off with no drunken floozy. Anyway, if he did, she'd sober up quicker than a duck on a June bug. Wouldn't take her anytime to find out all he knows is football and politics. *(pause)* That floozy would practically run by the courthouse and throw him out on his ear. *(She laughs.)*

MAMA. *(as she is drinking her wine)* Not right to talk about your husband like that. He makes a livin for ya...oughta show him more respect.

ACIA. Respect my ass! He's always been a bore. Now that he's mayor too, he's a egotistical bore.

RUTHIE ANN. *(getting a dig at ACIA)* Maybe he's just bein

a true patriot.

ACIA. Bein a patriot's got nothin to do with him stickin his head outta his office window askin me what I'm fixin to do. Plain embarrassin, is what it is.

MAMA. Shouldn't stay married to a man ya don't love.

ACIA. There's all kindsa love. One persons love don't have to be the same as somebody else's.

MAMA. *(being very cynical)* What kind is yours?

ACIA. I'm the kind that just lives it...*day by day,* cause I don't care nothin about the past and may not be here for the future...so I just live for today.

(The telephone rings.)

ACIA. There's Milton again, wonderin where I am.

RUTHIE ANN. *(Goes over to the phone and picks it up.)* Hello. *(pause)* Yeah, wait a minute. *(She holds out the phone to ACIA.)*

ACIA. See! Bug...bug...bug. I can't enjoy myself at all. I might just up and run off one of these days, before I go crazy. *(into the phone)* Yeah, whatta ya want? *(pause)* No. *(pause)* Cause we hadn't had our meetin yet. *(pause)* Sybil hadn't shown up, that's why. *(pause)* I'm not callin for any damned references. Go ahead and hire her if ya wantta...if not, forget it. *(pause)* Look! I don't care if she is a whore.

MAMA. Who's a whore?

RUTHIE ANN. Shh Mama, Acia's on the phone.

MAMA. I see she's on the phone. I wantta know who's a whore.

ACIA. *(into the phone)* Hold on a minute, Milton. *(She puts down the phone and goes to her purse and gets a cigarette and lights it, talking all the while to the ladies.)* The Butler girl applied for the waitress job at the cafe...Milton says she's a whore.

MAMA. *She* is a whore.

RUTHIE ANN. Mama!

MAMA. It's the God's truth. Been a whore since Pearl Harbor Day.

RUTHIE ANN. She was barely born then.

MAMA. Well, wasn't too much longer after that.

ACIA. *(back into the phone)* I'm back. *(pause)* Decide it for yourself. *(pause)* Hire the Butler girl if ya need her. *(pause)* Oh shit Milton, tell her not to wear short shorts. *(She slams down the phone. To the others.)* See what I gotta put up with. I swear I don't get any peace.

MAMA. *(nonchalantly)* It's not the Butler girls fault she's a whore. *(ACIA and RUTHIE ANN just look at her.)* Well, her Mama was a whore..and her Grandmama before that. It runs in the family...it's the family profession.

RUTHIE ANN. She's one of the nominees for Homecomin Queen.

MAMA. Lord Almighty, who nominated her?

RUTHIE ANN. *(Goes to where the nomination forms are and picks them up.)* Yeah, I'm right. Here's the vote she got. *(She waves it in the air.)*

ACIA. *(Runs over and grabs it from RUTHIE ANN.)* Let me see that. *(pause)* It's not signed.

RUTHIE ANN. *(being very magnanimous)* Never was any rules about havin'um signed. We gotta *consider* her, too.

MAMA. Not if it's not signed.

RUTHIE ANN. It wasn't in the rules, so it's legitimate. Anyway, I only got five votes here...three of these are outta town girls.

MAMA. I don't care. You can't pick Lois Butler as Homecomin Queen.

ACIA. Why not?

MAMA. Acia Darlin, you'd be the laughin stock of this whole town.

ACIA. Let'um laugh. It'd make her Mama happy... her Grandmama too. Can't ya just see the look on the men's faces when she rides in the parade...sittin up there on that float with pride...holdin her head high. *(thinking to herself)* and when the mayor has to place the crown on her head... *(drops what she's saying and begins to laugh)*

MAMA. You can't pick her, just cause it'd make the whoremongers unhappy and Milton a blitherin idiot.

ACIA. Yes we can.

RUTHIE ANN. *(not so magnanimous anymore)* We gotta consider her...not *pick* her.

ACIA. We'll see what Sybil has to say about it. *(She goes to the window and looks out.)* Wish to hell she'd get here. It'd be just like her to stop down at the drug store and stuff herself fatter on a chocolate malted.

RUTHIE ANN. But she's on a diet...

MAMA. *(interrupts)* Bet that's where she is. Ruthie Ann, call the drug store.

RUTHIE ANN. I'm not callin the drugstore. Why if she's there, she'd be embarrassed to tears.

MAMA. *(heads to the phone)* I'll do it. Don't bother me catchin her eatin somethin she's not suppose to. *(picks up the phone.)*

RUTHIE ANN. *(to ACIA)* See what you did. Now Mama is gonna embarrass Sybil.

ACIA. Serves her right. Keepin us waitin like this, while she stuffs herself on chocolate. *(pause)* Mama Wallace, you want some more wine?

RUTHIE ANN. Mama shouldn't have any more liquor, Acia.

MAMA. *(to RUTHIE ANN)* Who appointed you my tongue. *(to ACIA)* Pour me another one. *(into the phone)* Hello Mr. Black. *(She speaks up louder.)* Mr. Black, this is Mama Wallace here. *(Speaks even louder.)* I said, this is Mama Wallace here. *(to the girls)* Land sakes, that ole fool is deaf as a door nail. *(pause)* No Mr. Black, it's got nothin to do with the mail. Is Sybil Parker there? *(screams into the phone)* Sybil Parker! *(pause)* Thank ya Mr. Black. *(to the girls)* He went to get her. If he don't get himself a hearin aid... *(Holds out the phone to RUTHIE ANN.)* Here!

RUTHIE ANN. *(backs away)* No sir, you tracked her down.

ACIA. *(Grabs the phone from MAMA WALLACE and MAMA goes to drink more wine and study her dress pattern.)* Let me...why I'm gonna jump all over her as... *(into the phone)* Sybil, this is Acia...

RUTHIE ANN. Now, don't be too hard...

ACIA. *(into the phone)* What the hell are you doin there? *(pause)* Pantyhose? Sure, Sybil. Well, we just been sittin here twiddlin our thumbs, waitin on ya. *(pause)* You just get your butt over here, *right now*...oh, and Sybil, don't forget your pantyhose. *(She hangs up the phone.)* Now she'll have to buy herself a pair she don't need, for lyin like that. Why Ole Man Black never even heard of pantyhose.

He's still got nylons on his shelves from World War II.

(The telephone rings.)

MAMA. That phone is gettin down right irritatin.

ACIA. *(to RUTHIE ANN)* Milton's tryin to drive me crazy. Tell him I died and went to meet my maker. Be just like him to be jealous of the Lord.

RUTHIE ANN. *(as she picks up the phone)* I'm not lyin for you. *(She picks up the phone.)* Hello. *(pause)* Yeah, she's here all right.

ACIA. Damn you, Ruthie Ann.

RUTHIE ANN. *(with a smirk on her face)* It's for you Mama. It's Miss Elly.

ACIA. That was just real tacky.

MAMA. *(goes to the phone)* Hi Miss Elly. *(pause)* Been lookin at it. *(pause)* I'm bout ready to cut it out. *(pause)* We can use the dinin table. *(pause)* Oh, have you ever hit a wisteria bush with a shovel?

ACIA. *(to RUTHIE ANN)* A gardenin question?

RUTHIE ANN. It's some stupid thing she read in a book. They'll write anything anymore to sell a book.

MAMA. *(into the phone)* Yeah, come on. *(She hangs up the phone and to the girls.)* She's comin over and we're gonna cut out my dress. Clear this table off.

RUTHIE ANN. But it's set up for our meetin.

MAMA. Well, just unset it.

RUTHIE ANN. But I need this table to...

MAMA. You get this stuff offa here, right now. I'm gettin my scissors. *(She exits to the bedroom.)*

RUTHIE ANN. *(to ACIA)* Move those pictures...we'll use that. *(referring to the coffee table)* Once Mama makes up her mind, it is *made up,* and that's all there is to it. *(They remove everything from the table, except the sugar bowl and creamer, which they forget and leave.)*

ACIA. *(as she picks up the bowl of cookies)* Sybil shouldn't want any of these cookies...she'll be stuffed to the gills.

RUTHIE ANN. Better than *looped* to the gills.

ACIA. Why don't you ever let go...have some fun in life.

RUTHIE ANN. Life's not meant to be all fun...there is a serious...

ACIA. *(interrupts)* Don't go spoutin any of your 19th century philosophy to me. *(pause)* That's the very reason Harry ran off with another woman.

RUTHIE ANN. *(Gets very upset and runs over and grabs ACIA by the shoulders and shakes her.)* You take that back...take it back!

ACIA. *(pushes her away)* I'm takin nothin back! *(RUTHIE ANN goes to where the wash cloth is and gets it and sits down on the couch and puts it on her forehead and leans her head back and closes her eyes.)* You'd ever once...just once gone out to The Blue Moon with him, instead of waitin to preach your sermon on the mount...he might still be around.

RUTHIE ANN. *(Slowly lifts her head and takes the washcloth off and very sarcastically.)* Never saved his soul, that's for sure. *(pause)* He became a total bum hangin out there.

ACIA. You think anybody who gets a little pleasure outta livin is a bum. You like gloom and doom...it makes ya comfortable.

RUTHIE ANN. *(Jumps up from the couch and goes over to her.)* Where do you get off bein such an authority on Harry.

You hardly even knew him. *(Pause. Begins to wander aimlessly around the room.)* I knew what he needed...it wasn't whiskey either. *(pause)* Harry was a outcast in this town...his Daddy bein a Mexican. *(faces ACIA and direct to her)* Remember...*Half-breed Harry!*

ACIA. Well, with you bein the perfect little housewife, you probably didn't even notice things were changin and...

RUTHIE ANN. *(Not even hearing ACIA and continues to wander aimlessly around and almost to herself.)* My Mama threw a fit when I married him. Woulda thought he was from some other planet. She'd been happier, if I'd married Godzilla. To this day she still calls him a foreigner.

ACIA. Can't change everbody's attitude, but that doesn't mean...

RUTHIE ANN. Well...I'm not so dead set against drink as I used to be. When Harry comes back, I'll go out to The Blue Moon with him.

ACIA. *(laughs)* You hadn't heard a word I've said. *(pause)* There will be moss growin under your arms, before he takes you out to The Blue Moon.

RUTHIE ANN. You're dead wrong! Cause when he comes back to get his bowlin trophies...

ACIA. Harry, don't give a damn about no ole bowlin trophies.

RUTHIE ANN. He loved bowlin better than drinkin. There's a three-hundred trophy, packed away out there. *(pause)* A *three-hundred trophy.* That's perfect. No man's gonna walk off and forget somethin he did perfect.

ACIA. *(getting bored with the whole conversation.)* You're a fool sittin here cryin over somebody, who ain't cryin over you, and that's a fact.

Ruthie Ann. Harry ain't the cryin type.

Acia. I've seen him cry...more than once too.

Ruthie Ann. Course...he was drunk out there. All drunks get on cryin jags.

Acia. He wasn't drunk. Sometimes he got in a talkin mood and we'd sit around and...

Ruthie Ann. And what!

Acia. *(realizes she's said too much)* Gossip about life and what a bitch she is.

(Enter MAMA from the bedroom. She has her scissors and a pin cushion with some straight pins in it.)

Mama. I'm ready to cut out my dress. *(She looks at the table and sees the sugar and creamer and it makes her mad.)* I told you girls to get this stuff outta here. *(She goes over to the table and pushes it all into the floor.)*

Ruthie Ann. Oh, that's just great Mama. Now look what a mess you made.

Mama. When I tell you to do somethin girl, I intend for you to do it.

Acia. I'll get somethin to clean it up. *(She exits to the kitchen.)*

Ruthie Ann. *(to her mother)* You're actin like a baby.

Mama. I'm not the baby around here. I'm not still livin with my Mama.

Ruthie Ann. *(This hurts her feelings and she becomes very defensive.)* So, it finally comes out. You want me to move. *(pause)* Well, is that it?

Mama. You need a job first, Ruthie Ann. You've gotta

go to work.

 RUTHIE ANN. *(gets very upset)* Oh, I'll get a job all right and I'll get outta here...don't ya worry yourself none about that. *(pause)* You got a cruel streak in you Mama...you disguise it as stubborness. Does that make it easier for you to live with yourself?

(There's a knock at the door.)

 MAMA. That'll be Miss Elly...let her in.

 RUTHIE ANN. *(As she exits to the bedroom and looking at her Mother.)* This is your house, remember. *(She exits.)*

 MAMA. *(Goes to the door muttering to herself.)* Don't pay tryin to get kids to stand on their own two feet...they just gonna wind up kickin ya for it.

(She opens the door and enter MISS ELLY. She's wearing the same type of house dress as MAMA and is using a cane.)

 MAMA. Come on and get offa that leg for awhile. *(She leads her to a chair and helps her to sit down.)* Ya takin anything for the pain?

 ELLY. Some anacin, but it still aches like a sore tooth.

 MAMA. Well, me and Acia was just havin us some...

 ELLY. Acia? Is she here?

(Enter ACIA from the kitchen with a broom and a dustpan.)

 ACIA. Yes I am Miss Elly. How are ya?

 ELLY. Wasn't for my arthritis, I'd be dandy. *(Notices the

mess on the floor) What's all that?

ACIA. *(looks at MAMA, who says nothing)* Just a little acci-
dent, that's all. *(She begins to clean up the mess.)*

MAMA. *(Gets her material and takes it over to ELLY.)* This
sure is a pretty color, ain't it?

ELLY. You're gonna be glad ya got this light weight cotton too, come next month. *(pause)* Remember that ole cat
I had, bout this color.

ACIA. *(as though ELLY is telling a big yarn)* Now Miss Elly,
you didn't have any pink cat.

ELLY. Amy was this color...wasn't she Mama?

MAMA. Almost was...she was some odd cat.

ELLY. *(remembering and laughing)* Was afraid of rugs...-
wouldn't walk on one for love nor money.

MAMA. *(remembering too)* Would jump straight up in the
air when she saw a rug.

ELLY. Amy went completely berserk.

MAMA. We took her to Ole Doc Andrews...told him
how crazy she was actin.

ELLY. Asked me what I was feedin her.

MAMA. Cat food, Miss Elly says.

ELLY. No wonder she's flippin out, Doc Andrews said.
Don't ever feed a cat...cat food. *(pause)* Organ meats! A
cat needs organ meats...heart, brains, kidneys, liver.

MAMA. *(to ELLY)* How much did we spend on organ
meats for Amy?

ELLY. Twenty dollars.

MAMA. *(to ACIA)* She still jumped straight up in the air,
when she saw a rug.

ACIA. I read somewhere, that some kindsa rugs
shock cats.

ELLY. You mean to tell me, that I spent twenty dollars for organ meats, for nothin.

ACIA. Most likely.

MAMA. Between Ole Doc Andrews for animals and Ole Doc Cox for people...

ELLY. They don't have a brain between'um.

MAMA. *(to ELLY)* I'm thinkin about havin a gathered neckline on my dress.

ELLY. Why? The ruffles are pretty.

ACIA. Miss Elly, ruffles are just too babyfied.

ELLY. Well, maybe so.

MAMA. *(to ELLY)* You want some wine?

ELLY. If it'll go straight to my knee, instead of my brain, bring it on.

MAMA. I'll get you a glass. *(to ACIA)* I'll throw that out. *(She takes the broom and dustpan and starts to exit.)*

ACIA. Need any help?

MAMA. I can manage. *(She exits to the kitchen.)*

ELLY. *(Gets up and begins to wander around the room, walking with the cane.)* Can't sit still too long...this knee gets stiff as a board. *(pause)* Saw you in Athens on Wednesday with another man. Who was he? *(ACIA doesn't answer.)* Wasn't from around these parts. Milton's liable to get upset, if he hears about you and another man.

ACIA. *(laughs)* That's what I like about you, Miss Elly. You're *direct,* that's for sure...but you should mind your own business, before somebody starts mindin yours. *(pause)* You know how the Coleridge Rumor Factory works. Like the product put out about you and Mama Wallace, that's been goin around for years.

ELLY. Never was bothered by rumors. Figure folks

who put out such things, will come to no good end.

ACIA. Sure wouldn't want such things put out about me and a strange man in Athens.

ELLY. Said I wasn't bothered by rumors. You and a strange man's a fact...saw it with my own eyes.

ACIA. When Coleridge gets a hold of it, it'll just be a rumor.

ELLY. That's likely. *(pause)* But won't ever be just a rumor to me.

ACIA. *(almost a threat)* I wouldn't want things to get ugly here, but if you start...

ELLY. *(back at her)* Start what? *(ACIA says nothing.)* Come on girl, if you got somethin to say, speak up. I don't respect people who beat around the bush.

ACIA. *(Thinks about it a second and then laughs.)* I got nothin more to say, Miss Elly.

ELLY. In that case, where's the wine?

ACIA. Over there. *(Goes to where the wine is and picks it up.)* We gotta dead soldier here.

ELLY. Gotta a jug on the sideboard in my dinin room...go get it. Mind ya don't step on my portulaca, planted by the front steps either.

ACIA. I'll jump high as a elephant's eye, Miss Elly. *(She exits out the front door.)*

(MAMA comes back into the room, carrying a glass.)

MAMA. *(takes the glass over to ELLY)* Where's she goin?

ELLY. My house to get another jug. That ones empty. *(pause)* Ruthie Ann's not home?

MAMA. She's in there poutin.

ELLY. What about?

MAMA. Life, I guess. I want her to stop livin in a dream and she don't wantta wake up.

ELLY. Just gonna have to shake her a little harder. *(pause)* Acia was just down-right forward bout those rumors regardin us.

MAMA. Women can't be friends and love each other anymore, without everbody thinkin there's somethin wrong.

ELLY. We're livin in troubled times. Everthing's suspect now. *(pause)* Remember when we use to go to those barn dances...our husbands would just sit there, like bumps on a log. We'd get up and dance and dance and dance...just you and me...glidin all over the floor. *(pause)* We was the best couple in Freestone County.

MAMA. Really a shame...cryin shame is what it is. Ole friends can't dance together anymore and walk along holdin hands.

ELLY. Concerns me some about Acia foolin around on Milton.

MAMA. She don't think he's got the balls to do nothin about it.

ELLY. Don't take balls...just a gun, that's all.

MAMA. Maybe you oughta talk to her.

ELLY. Tried. She told me to mind my own business. *(pause)* She might not can find that wine. I best go help her.

MAMA. You stay offa your knee...I'll go.

(As MAMA starts to exit, the phone rings.)

MAMA. Get that...I'll be right back. *(She exits and ELLY goes to the phone.)*

ELLY. *(into the phone)* Hello. *(pause)* She ain't here. *(pause)* Calm down, she went to my house. *(pause)* Who do you think it is...it's Miss Elly. *(pause)* Don't you go swearin at me, Milton Darlin. You best mind your manners, fore I come over there and...Hello. *(She slams down the phone.)*

(During the conversation on the phone, RUTHIE ANN has come back into the room and is mopping her forehead with another wash rag.)

ELLY. That man is a total son-of-a-somethin. He hung up on me.

RUTHIE ANN. *(As she sits down on the couch and again leans her head back and places the wash cloth over her eyes.)* He sure bothers Acia, don't he?

ELLY. Don't give her much breathin space, that's for sure. *(pause)* Ruthie Ann, what are you and your Mama fightin about?

RUTHIE ANN. *(Takes the rag off and looks at MISS ELLY.)* She told me to get outta here and go to work.

ELLY. Why don't ya? Don't ya ever want your own place again?

RUTHIE ANN. Sure I do Miss Elly, but when Harry comes back...

ELLY. I'd give up on Harry by now.

RUTHIE ANN. Everbody wants me to just give up on him. *Well, I'm not! (Again she leans her head back and places the wash cloth over her eyes.)* And Mama...Mama actually said she thought I should work in a Honky Tonk.

ELLY. What Honky Tonk?

RUTHIE ANN. The Blue Moon...Milton's lookin for a waitress.

ELLY. I been out there.

RUTHIE ANN. *(sits straight up)* Miss Elly!

ELLY. He's got it set up real nice like. There's cloths on the tables...candles...even a printed menu...pictures on the walls...

RUTHIE ANN. Naked women!

ELLY. Picture I saw was of Eisenhower and Churchill... they wasn't naked.

RUTHIE ANN. He probably hides the naked women, till the rowdy bunch gets there.

ELLY. Ya know, I hear on a real good night, his waitress makes around 15 or 20 dollars in tips.

RUTHIE ANN. She does? *(ELLY shakes her head yes.)* Well, I'd have to think long and hard on it.

ELLY. Best not think too long or the job'll be gone.

(ACIA and MAMA enter from the front porch and ACIA is carrying a big gallon jug of wine.)

ACIA. I didn't step on your portulaca...we got us a bigger soldier too. Gonna take alot to kill him.

RUTHIE ANN. *(back into her pious attitude)* Ya'll just gonna set around here all afternoon and drink liquor?

MAMA. We're gonna cut out my dress, too.

RUTHIE ANN. I can see I'm in for a good time...watchin two drunk ole women mess up some material and two young ones, pick a whore for Homecomin Queen.

ELLY. *(to MAMA)* What's she talkin about?

MAMA. Butler girl got a nomination for Homecomin Queen and Acia wants to crown her.

ELLY. *(laughs)* Is that a fact, Acia?

ACIA. Why not? Might be the only honor she ever receives in her whole lifetime. Everbody should have one pleasant thing happen to'um, so they can reflect on it in their old age.

ELLY. Sounds fittin to me. *(pause)* Let's have some of this. *(referring to the wine and to RUTHIE ANN)* Come on and have some...might even like it.

ACIA. *(winks at ELLY)* I'll get her a glass. *(She runs to the kitchen.)*

RUTHIE ANN. But Acia, I don't... *(to the others)* I don't normally drink...drinkin's a real sin.

ELLY. *(Placating her, as she takes a big swig of her own wine.)* We all know how bad it is for ya.

RUTHIE ANN. But maybe the Lord will forgive me, cause this has been one bad day.

(ACIA comes back into the room with a glass and goes over to ELLY, who pours RUTHIE ANN a glass.)

RUTHIE ANN. *(Feeling sorry for herself and needing an excuse to drink.)* What with Mama orderin me outta the house and this headache...

MAMA. Never did nothin of the kind. I said getta job, first.

RUTHIE ANN. *(taking the wine and drinking it)* I'm not trained for nothin. I don't know how to do anything. I'm a forty year ole nothin.

ACIA. I didn't know ya wanted to work.

MAMA. She don't!

RUTHIE ANN. I do so, but at what. What's a forty year ole nothing to do.

ACIA. Take the waitress job at the Blue Moon and get Milton offa my back with the Butler girl.

ELLY. She workin there?

ACIA. Applied for the job. Milton's caught between a rock and a hard place. He needs her, but don't wantta hire her...if he had another applicant.

MAMA. He's got one. Ruthie Ann, you're gonna apply.

RUTHIE ANN. But Mama...

ACIA. *(trying to convince her)* You could bring some gentility to that place.

RUTHIE ANN. I could?

ACIA. Culture! That's exactly what you got and what The Blue Moon needs.

ELLY. And unless there's a educated person around who knows who they are...a picture of Eisenhower and Churchill, don't mean nothin. *(ACIA and MAMA look at her and she returns the look with a...I know what I'm doing look.)*

RUTHIE ANN. *(is about taken in by it all)* Well?

MAMA. And don't forget you'd be gettin paid for it too.

ACIA. *(looks at her watch)* I don't know what happened to Sybil. She must a overdosed on chocolate malteds.

(The telephone rings.)

ACIA. It'll be Milton. This must be the hundredth time

he's called.

ELLY. Hundred and one. Called a minute ago...talked smart-mouthed to me, too.

RUTHIE ANN. *(goes over and picks up the phone)* Hello Milton. *(pause)* Cause you're the only one drivin us crazy, callin here ever other minute. *(pause)* Don't ya scream at me. *(pause)* We hadn't had our meetin, cause Sybil hadn't shown up yet. *(pause)* What the devil is she doin down there? *(pause)* Next time you call our house, act like a gentlemen...we're ladies here. *(hands the phone to ACIA)* He's mad as a wet hen.

ACIA. *(takes the phone)* Who gives a damn. I'm used to his temper. *(into the phone)* Whatta ya want? *(pause)* How did you expect her references to turn out? Ya said yourself, she's a whore...forget her anyway, I about got Ruthie Ann talked into bein your new waitress. *(pause)* I know she's got no experience but she's not a whore.

RUTHIE ANN. See Mama, even Milton knows I can't do nothin.

ACIA. *(into the phone)* We'll just have our meetin without Sybil. I'll be there in fifteen minutes or so. *(She hangs up the phone and to RUTHIE ANN.)* You'll get the job...if ya want it. *(pause)* Well, do ya?

MAMA. She wants it. Thank you for your concern for Ruthie Ann's well bein.

ELLY. Do her good to mix and mingle.

RUTHIE ANN. I'm happy ya'll consider it your duty to see to it that I'm gainfully employed in a place where I can get screwed once in awhile. *(They all laugh, except RUTHIE ANN.)* Milton said he saw Sybil down at the dry goods store awhile back.

ACIA. Buyin herself a pair of pantyhose, was what she was doin.

ELLY. Let's get to this pattern. I wantta get home in time to fix me some fried okra for supper.

MAMA. Got somethin I wantta do myself, before dark. *(They both get up and get the pattern. They take it apart and begin to lay it out on the table and arrange the material and start to generally get ready to cut out the dress.)*

ACIA. We're gonna have to forget this meetin, cause...

(SYBIL finally comes lumbering through the door. She's a fat lady and is dressed in a sacky dress. She has on a sweater and is carrying a few books and a paper sack.)

SYBIL. *(upon entering)* It's hot as Hades out there. I bout had a stroke walkin over here.

ACIA. What route did ya take...The Polar Route. We been waitin here a solid hour for you.

RUTHIE ANN. *(to SYBIL)* Why you wearin a sweater in this heat?

SYBIL. Helps to burn off some of my carbohydrates.

ACIA. We're drinkin wine. Want some, or are you too full of chocolate?

SYBIL. I don't know what you mean. *(pause)* Does wine have carbohydrates in it?

ACIA. *(exasperated with SYBIL)* How the shit should I know. I don't have to read diet books.

RUTHIE ANN. All liquor has carbohydrates *(thinks to herself)* or all liquor don't...it's one or the other.

SYBIL. Well, which is it?

ACIA. Do you want some or not.

SYBIL. Suppose a small glass won't hurt. *(RUTHIE ANN pours her a glass.)* Help to kill my appetite before supper. *(pause)* I can only have two-hundred more calories today. Mostly green vegetables and such.

ACIA. *(winking at RUTHIE ANN)* What ya got in the sack?

SYBIL. Pantyhose. Told ya I needed to get...

ACIA. *(grabs for the sack)* Let's see what kind ya got.

SYBIL. *(Tries to keep the sack away from her.)* But they're just plain ole pantyhose...

ACIA. I wantta see'um anyway. *(She takes the sack away from her and takes out the pantyhose and they are a very small size.)* Sybil Parker, these here pantyhose ain't gonna fit over your *feet,* much less your *ass.*

SYBIL. *(Grabs the pantyhose back from ACIA.)* Just goes to show what you know, Acia Darlin...cause that's one size fits all.

ACIA. When they talk about one size fittin all, they ain't talkin about cows.

RUTHIE ANN. You stop insultin her.

ACIA. It's the truth, can't help if it comes out a insult. *(pause)* I been insulted by the truth alot in my lifetime.

MAMA. Anybody ever call you a cow? *(pause)* Sorry Sybil.

ACIA. No, but I been called a bitch.

RUTHIE ANN. *(smirking)* Is that a truth.

SYBIL. I'd rather be called a bitch than a cow, even if it was the truth. *(pause)* Anyway, I'm not gonna be a cow much longer. I've already lost 15 pounds.

RUTHIE ANN. How much more ya got to go?

SYBIL. 35 more pounds and I'll be at a good weight.

ACIA. Good weight for what? Wrestlin a bear. You need to lose 50 more and while you been stuffin yourself on chocolate, Milton has flat blown our meetin away... cause I got no more time to set here and pick a Homecomin Queen.

RUTHIE ANN. Why don't we meet tomorrow?

MAMA. *(to RUTHIE ANN)* If ya meet here, unpack some of your own things.

RUTHIE ANN. No need to. Nobody ate any cookies or...

SYBIL. Cookies! You got some cookies?

MAMA. Over in that bowl. *(points to where the cookies are)* Chocolate chip...homemade too.

ACIA. *(to SYBIL)* You only have two-hundred more calories to go today, remember.

SYBIL. One little ole chocolate chip cookies not gonna hurt. I'll just eat less green vegetable for supper. *(She goes to the bowl and proceeds to eat three or four.)*

ACIA. *(just shakes her head)* What time ya wantta meet tomorrow?

MAMA. Make it nightime, cause I wantta finish my dress and you can't use this table.

RUTHIE ANN. Well, that's fine by us...be *selfish!*

ACIA. *(to RUTHIE ANN)* Come over in the mornin and talk to Milton about the job at The Blue Moon. I'll call ya and let ya know the time.

SYBIL. *(almost chokes on a cookie)* The Blue Moon! Ruthie Ann, you can't work at The Blue Moon.

MAMA. Hush your mouth, Sybil.

ELLY. Tend to your own knittin.

SYBIL. *(looks perplexed)* Did I say somethin wrong? *(shrugs her shoulders and to ACIA)* Can you give me a lift downtown?

ACIA. If you wasn't so fat, walkin one block wouldn't tire ya out...and you ate more than one cookie, too.

SYBIL. *(defiant and goes and picks up another cookie)* Yeah, and I'm gonna have one for the road.

ACIA. You gonna stay fat all your natural born life, cause you got no will power.

SYBIL. Not about eatin, but I do about other things.

ACIA. Like what?

SYBIL. *(trying to come up with something)* Well...ah...hum. I can do without sex!

ACIA. Sybil Parker, if you'd rather eat a chocolate chip cookie than have sex, you deserve to stay fat...come on. Bye everbody.

SYBIL. *(As she is eating the cookie.)* Yeah, bye. *(They exit.)*

RUTHIE ANN. *(at the door)* See ya'll tomorrow. *(She closes the door.)*

MAMA. It's about dark Miss Elly, let's quit. *(pause)* I'll be right back. *(She exits through the kitchen door.)*

RUTHIE ANN. *(to ELLY)* You sure there's no pictures of naked ladies at The Blue Moon?

ELLY. *(shakes her head yes)* Food's good too.

RUTHIE ANN. All this time I thought...it's surprisin is what it is.

ELLY. Life's full of surprises. That's what the Lord uses to make it fun for us to get up in the mornin.

RUTHIE ANN. Wish he had a surprise for me in the mornin...like Harry comin back to get his trophies.

ELLY. Lord don't work on wishes. Take Harry's trophies to him.

RUTHIE ANN. But I don't know where he's even...

ELLY. He's over in Athens, shacked up with that woman.

RUTHIE ANN. *(This comes as a total surprise.)* Athens! How do you know that?

ELLY. Acia told me...told me along time ago.

RUTHIE ANN. How would *she* know Harry's over in Athens?

ELLY. *(without thinking and it will be a very bad mistake)* Ask your Mama. I'm not gonna be the one to tell ya.

RUTHIE ANN. *(tries to find out more)* What are you sayin, Miss Elly? *(At this point, ELLY realizes she's said way too much and she doesn't answer.)* I wantta know what you're sayin. *(Again ELLY says nothing.)* Are you tellin me...are you sayin...

(At this point MAMA comes back in the room with a shovel and stands in the background.)

RUTHIE ANN. You're not tellin me...there was somethin between Harry and Acia. *(ELLY makes a pathetic effort to shrug it off, but says nothing.)* Well, answer me!

ELLY. *(Sees how serious the situation is now and is going to try and ease the blow some.)* Now...ah, well, it wasn't nothin too serious Ruthie Ann, but...

RUTHIE ANN. *(voice raised) That* is what you are sayin. I don't believe you. You're lyin to me. Why would you lie like that?

MAMA. Don't call Miss Elly a liar...*they was carryin on.*

(This hits RUTHIE ANN like a bomb and totally decimates her.) If you hadn't a been so wrapped up in being the perfect housewife, ya woulda seen what was goin on...right under your own nose.

RUTHIE ANN. *(Can't believe her mother is telling her something like this.)* Why are you tellin me this, Mama? Why?

MAMA. Cause you gotta wake up and I gotta shake ya to do it. Now, that's the way it was. I got no reason to tell ya different. *(RUTHIE ANN stands there as though in a stupor and MAMA feels bad about hitting her so hard with the news and goes over and tries to put her arm around her and RUTHIE ANN turns away from her.)* I'm sorry to shatter your dream, but you can't spend the rest of your life asleep.

ELLY. *(goes over to RUTHIE ANN)* I'd like ya to forgive me, Ruthie Ann, I just spoke without... *(RUTHIE ANN turns her back on MISS ELLY and walks out of the room into the bedroom.)*

ELLY. *(to MAMA)* Thinkin...I spoke without thinkin.

MAMA. Learned somethin from that book you gave me...let's go try it out. *(They exit out the front door with MAMA carrying the shovel. RUTHIE ANN comes back into the room and has another wash cloth with her and is wiping the back of her neck and she looks toward the door and shouts.)*

RUTHIE ANN. Why did you do that to me, Mama! Take away my hope! *(She goes over to the wine and pours herself a glass.)* My husband and my best friend. *(She takes the wine and goes to the window and leans up against the sill, sipping the wine and crying, while looking out the window.)* Look at that ole fool woman out there...beatin that bush with that shovel. Hurting it bad, just like she hurt me. *(She continues to cry.)*

CURTAIN
End of Act One

ACT TWO
SCENE ONE

*As the lights come up, MAMA is sitting at the dining table in her
   robe and is drinking a cup of coffee. There's a knock at the
   door and MISS ELLY just comes on in. She's dressed in gardening clothes, wearing a baggy pair of slacks, a loose-fitting
   blouse and an old floppy hat.*

ELLY. Mornin Mama. I'm headed to Athens this afternoon...wantta go?

MAMA. I best finish my dress. *(pause)* Wantta cup of
coffee?

ELLY. Yeah, I'll take one. *(MAMA gets up and goes to the
sideboard and gets her a cup. She brings it back to the table and
pours her a cup and they both sit down.)* Looks like this dress is
comin along really good.

MAMA. Pretty much so.

ELLY. Ruthie Ann still asleep?

MAMA. *(shakes her head yes)* Heard her tossin and turnin
all night long.

ELLY. Shame I let it slip like that.

MAMA. Just as well she found out. *(pause)* For the life of
me, I can't figure out how any woman can get so wrapped
up in a man.

ELLY. Don't you really know why Ruthie Ann is so
crazy about Harry?

MAMA. *(can't even begin to guess)* No I really don't.

ELLY. He's about the handsomest man I ever laid eyes on.

MAMA. *(Has never noticed Harry is handsome, because she is so prejudiced .)* Harry? He was not!

ELLY. Was too.

MAMA. He was a foreigner.

ELLY. We're talkin about Harry like he's already passed on.

MAMA. Has so far as I'm concerned.

ELLY. What about Ruthie Ann?

MAMA. *(Begins to think about Harry.)* You really think Harry's handsome?

ELLY. *(shakes her head yes)* Dark wavy hair...big brown eyes.

MAMA. Handsome is as handsome does...I say.

ELLY. I used to go by their house and he'd be workin in his roses...no shirt...beautiful bronze chest. *(pause)* Yes sir, I ogled him on more than one occasion.

MAMA. *(gently scolding her)* Elly. *(pause)* Harry's roses was pretty. *(pause)* But Ruthie Ann shoulda never married him...her knowin I didn't like him.

ELLY. You're kinda disappointed she didn't turn out like you...ain't ya?

MAMA. Yeah I am, cause I'm like my Mama and my Mama's Mama.

ELLY. It don't always work out the way we want it to.

MAMA. When I gave birth to her and she was layin next to me, all snuggled up warm and cozy like, I smiled to myself thinkin...she's gonna take after me when she gets big.

ELLY. She does some.

MAMA. Not at all. No sir Elly, not at all. *(pause)* You love it...care for it...take it's little hand and raise it in the way you think it should go, and then it up and turns on ya. *(pause)* Or worse yet...it moves back in with ya when it gets big.

ELLY. *(laughs)* She'll be gettin her own place soon.

MAMA. Can't be soon enough for me. I want her to get all that stuff outta my garage. I don't even have room out there to piddle around anymore. *(pause)* This house ain't big enough for two women.

ELLY. No house is. *(pause)* Remember the time Sister came and spent the *whole summer* with me...the summer of 55, I think it was.

MAMA. Was the summer of 56. *(pause)* I remember cause it was the year I had my operation.

ELLY. Are you sure?

MAMA. Fall of 56, was when I went in for my female surgery.

ELLY. Slow as molasses...Sister was.

MAMA. That surgery almost killed me.

ELLY. It took her five solid hours to cook a meal.

MAMA. Suffer...Lord how I suffered. *(pause)* You griped about your Sister all summer long.

ELLY. Well, it'd be 10 o'clock at night fore she put supper on the table...by then I was nearly starved to death. *(pause)* You was in real bad shape for awhile there.

MAMA. Pain...I thought I was strong as a ox, till I had my surgery.

ELLY. Turtle...Sister was slow as a turtle.

MAMA. I told Doctor Cox...it'll be a cold day in hell

fore you get to cut on me again.

ELLY. I told Sister...I'll do the cookin.

MAMA. She flat took over your kitchen stove.

ELLY. Gotta earn my keep, she kept sayin. *(pause)* You was flat of your back along time.

MAMA. Hadn't recovered from that female surgery yet.

ELLY. Hungry...Lord, I stayed hungry the whole summer of 55.

MAMA. Agony...I was in pure D agony the whole fall of 56.

ELLY. You sure that's when it was?

MAMA. I'm not liable to forget when I was tortured the most in my lifetime.

ELLY. *(thinks about her sisters visit)* Come to think of it...I believe it was 56. *(pause)* When Brother-In-Law came to get Sister, I didn't give him time to get outta the car. I shoved her and her bags in the front seat, waved goodbye and was back in the house with the door bolted, fore they got outta the driveway. *(They both laugh.)*

MAMA. Fish and visitors, both start to smell after a couple a days.

ELLY. To high heaven. *(pause)* Mama, we're just set in our ways.

MAMA. Suppose so, but I just like bein by myself. *(pause)* You know, I never get bored with myself.

ELLY. Me neither. I can think of a million things to do. Work in my yard.

MAMA. Piddle in my garage.

ELLY. Crochet.

MAMA. Make me a new dress.

ELLY. Sit on my front porch, just watchin the world walk by.

MAMA. Ruthie Ann sleeps all the time. That's gotta be down-right borin.

ELLY. Sleepin her troubles away, is what she's doin. *(pause)* You need to have a heart to heart talk with your daughter.

MAMA. Conversin with Ruthie Ann is like pullin teeth.

ELLY. But you know she's hurtin bad findin out about Harry and Acia like that.

MAMA. Well, I'm just hopin she'll cry it out and then sweep it under the rug and forget it.

ELLY. Have you ever thought if she'd married Roy Black, things mighta been different?

MAMA. Don't know why you'd say that. Never have liked him either. *(pause)* Stuck-up...conceited, and Lord knows what about, cause he's homely as sin.

ELLY. He ain't so homely.

MAMA. Elly, he's got ears like a rabbit and teeth too. *(pause)* With all the Black's money, wouldn't ya a thought they'd done somethin for that poor homely things appearance.

ELLY. Cheap...The Blacks are just flat-out cheap.

MAMA. Don't I know it. That's why Ole Man Black don't buy himself a hearin aid, he'd rather be deaf than spend a dime. *(pause)* Rumor has it that when Doctor Cox cut off both Mrs. Black's breasts, Ole Man Black was too cheap to buy her any good falsies.

ELLY. I heard she got her a pair over at The Goodwill in Birmingham. Poor ole Thing, and Roy turned out to be just like his Ole Daddy...a *hoarder. (pause)* You oughta see his house. He's got junk piled clean up to the ceilin. Iron bedsteads, side-boards, ole pie safes, glass...lots a glass...depression, carnival, fiesta ware...

MAMA. You think he'd sell any of it? *(shakes her head no)* I offered him 25 dollars for a piece of carnival from Ole Lady Perkins estate.

ELLY. He wouldn't take it?

MAMA. *(shakes her head no)* He likes clutter. *(pause)* Some night I hope all that clutter falls down right on top of him.

ELLY. Don't you bet his house is just loaded with rats, roaches...

MAMA. *(shakes her head yes)* I bet they have a field day knawin on all that clutter. *(pause)* Least Harry wasn't a hoarder. Bought Ruthie Ann nice things too. He even bought me a present one time. Knew he wasn't welcome in my house, so he left it on the front porch.

ELLY. *(confronts MAMA with her prejudice)* You ever feel bad about bein so mean to Harry, just cause he was part Mexican?

MAMA. *(starts to deny it)* I didn't do it cause... *(ELLY looks at her and then MAMA owns up to it.)* Between you and me...sometimes. *(pause)* Guess one of these days I'll have to answer to it.

ELLY. What's your answer gonna be?

MAMA. Don't have one. Gonna throw myself on the Lord's mercy and ask him to forgive me.

ELLY. Could ask Harry.

MAMA. Naw, it's too late for me and Harry. *(pause)* Besides, after all's said and done...I still feel the same way.

ELLY. Knowin it's not right?

MAMA. Even knowin.

ELLY. I better go weed my flower bed. *(pause)* You talk to Ruthie Ann, OK?

MAMA. She won't listen.

ELLY. Make her listen.

MAMA. I'll try, but it won't do any good. *(pause)* You wouldn't have weeds in your portulaca if you'd planted it in pots.

ELLY. You tellin me how to grow portulaca?

MAMA. Does better in pots, bet my gardenin book says so. *(She goes and gets the book and begins to thumb through it.)* No portulaca in here.

ELLY. Look up moss rose.

MAMA. Moss rose ain't in here either. Where'd you get this gardenin book?

ELLY. Got it free with a bag of fertilizer.

MAMA. That's food for thought. Wonder if this here book is fact or bullshit.

(Enter RUTHIE ANN from the bedroom. She's dressed in a robe and house shoes. She goes to the sideboard and pours herself a cup of coffee and then goes to the dining table and sits down and proceeds to just stare into her cup.)

ELLY. It's fact. I've used that same book ever spring for the last two years.

MAMA. Then, why do you have weeds?

ELLY. Lord puts some weeds in everbodys garden.

MAMA. *(looks at RUTHIE ANN)* Mornin Ruthie Ann. *(RUTHIE ANN says nothing.)*

ELLY. Ruthie Ann, I'm sorry about yesterday. *(Again RUTHIE ANN says nothing but continues to stare into her cup.)*

MAMA. *(gently scolding her)* Miss Elly's talkin to ya.

RUTHIE ANN. I hear her talkin.

MAMA. *(again very nice)* You gonna accept her apology? *(RUTHIE ANN just stares at both of them and then proceeds to stare again in the cup.)*

ELLY. *(to MAMA)* Sure there's nothin you need from Athens?

MAMA. Not that I can think of.

ELLY. Well, better get started workin in my flower beds fore the sun get too high.

MAMA. *(As she walks her to the door and steps out onto the front porch.)* Weed killer, you need to get you some weed killer.

ELLY. *(from the outside)* Pluck up...you've gotta pluck up weeds.

(As they are both outside, the phone rings and RUTHIE ANN just sits at the table and doesn't answer it, the phone continues.)

MAMA. Ruthie Ann, I know you can hear this phone a ringin. *(As she comes to answer it.)*

RUTHIE ANN. I can't hear nothin this mornin. I feel like I've died and gone to hell.

MAMA. *(picks up the phone)* Hello. *(pause)* Yeah, hold on a minute Acia. *(She puts her hand over the phone.)* She wants to talk to you.

RUTHIE ANN. Tell her I'm sick in bed with the flu.

MAMA. She knows you ain't got any flu. You wasn't the

least bit sick yesterday.

RUTHIE ANN. Tell her I got the gallopin flu or somethin, cause I'm not talkin to her.

MAMA. *(back into the phone)* She's in the bathtub right now. *(pause)* What time did he wantta talk to her? *(pause)* I'll tell her. *(pause)* O.K. I'll have her call ya back then. *(She hangs up the phone.)*

RUTHIE ANN. Shouldn't a told her that. She's gonna be thinkin I'm awful clean by the end of the day, when I don't get outta the tub and return her call.

MAMA. Gonna avoid her the rest of your life? *(RUTHIE ANN still continues to stare into the cup.)* Maybe you oughta talk to her.

RUTHIE ANN. *(Swings around in her chair and faces her mother dead on.)* What should I say to her Mama? How did you like sleepin with my husband? Was he good?

MAMA. *(Throws up her hands in a gesture of futility.)* You're makin too big a thing outta this whole affair.

RUTHIE ANN. Shake me a little harder, Mama...make sure I'm awake. *(pause)* An affair everbody knew about, but me.

MAMA. Everbody didn't know about it. Wasn't any ongoin thing, either.

RUTHIE ANN. How'd you find out?

MAMA. Sybil told me.

RUTHIE ANN. Sybil! *(pause)* Guess she told Miss Elly, too. Told everbody it seems, *but me. (pause)* Well... well...my two best friends. Ain't that a laugh. A snake in the grass and a pig in the poke! *(pause)* And you...*you* shoulda told me about this sooner. I blame you for not tellin me things I need to know, before they fester to eat me up alive.

MAMA. Now, don't you go puttin this on me!

RUTHIE ANN. Oh, but I do! You hate me cause I'm weak and worthless, but you never raised me to be nothin else. How'd you expect me to turn out.

MAMA. Never said you was worthless.

RUTHIE ANN. Don't have to say it, Mama. Shows on your face when ya look at me.

MAMA. That's not so.

RUTHIE ANN. You never prepared me for the fight Mama, but you think it's character building to hit somebody full force...never mind they wasn't prepared. *(pause)* You never prepared me for nothin. Why until I was 15 years old, I thought ya got pregnant by a boy feelin around with your breast.

MAMA. *(Feels some guilt as she never told RUTHIE ANN the facts of life.)* Sex wasn't discussed in those days.

RUTHIE ANN. But I needed to know. *(pause)* I remember the day I made that fool statement about breasts. We was eatin our lunch out on the front yard of the school grounds. There was Acia, Sybil, Lucy Bates and me...we was talkin about boys and I confided that I thought I might be pregnant, cause I had let Roy Black touch my left breast. Why they all about choked to death on their tuna fish sandwiches. Tears of laughter rolled down their cheeks and I sat there not knowin what was even goin on.

MAMA. *(on the defense)* Not my fault ya let Roy Black play with your breast.

RUTHIE ANN. When Acia told me how ya really got pregnant, I felt like I'd been kicked by a mule.

MAMA. *(still defensive)* Woulda thought you'd been relieved, less you'd let him play with somethin else.

RUTHIE ANN. Make light of it, Mama...it eases your conscience some I'm sure. You shoulda told me about Harry and Acia *sooner.*

MAMA. Saw no point to it.

RUTHIE ANN. You see no point to anything that upsets your applecart.

MAMA. Knew Harry would leave someday and then when ya found out about him and Acia, it wouldn't be so hard on ya.

RUTHIE ANN. You knew Harry would leave...did ya? And you was gonna save me sufferin...was ya? *(pause)* You're a coward Mama...that's what you are and you got you're ole applecart goin one way, cause you don't want nothin to spill it over and that's all there is to it.

MAMA. Maybe I made some mistakes...did it thinkin I was doin right.

RUTHIE ANN. Well, you was dead wrong.

MAMA. Harry wasn't near good enough for ya. *(pause)* He's a foreigner.

RUTHIE ANN. He's an American. Born and raised here.

MAMA. He's not white.

RUTHIE ANN. The way you've talked all these years, you'd a thought Harry was from Mars or somewhere.

MAMA. Better he be a green Martian in Freestone County than a brown Mexican.

RUTHIE ANN. You're a bigot.

MAMA. I believe in marryin your own kind...if that makes me a bigot, then so be it. *(pause)* I'm proud to be an

American and proud of my name...*Wallace.*

RUTHIE ANN. I know ya hate my name.

MAMA. Don't hate it. It's just not American. *Castro!* What kinda name is that? Why that's some dictator's name in one of those foreign countries.

RUTHIE ANN. You're gonna go to your grave thinkin one way...*your way. (pause)* I pity ya for it.

MAMA. Don't pity me girl. I've never felt sorry for myself and I don't need you to do it for me. Never needed any man to be my whole world either. *(pause)* We all gotta get through life our way...prepared or not. *(pause)* You best talk to Acia about Harry. *She* knew him better than *you* ever did.

RUTHIE ANN. *(Turns on her mother with a vengence.)* I lived with Harry for twenty years and you're tellin me *I didn't know him! (pause)* You're crazy ole lady!

MAMA. *(Runs over to her and grabs her by the shoulders and begins to shake her.)* Don't you dare talk to me like that, Girl. Now I'm tellin ya like it is and it's gotta be said. You've gotta see it for yourself and get yourself together.

RUTHIE ANN. *(jerks away from her mother)* Oh, I see it all right. I am together. *(pause)* Why are you tryin to hurt me like this? Why? I intend to forgive Harry and Acia and when he comes back...

MAMA. *(A this point MAMA and RUTHIE ANN will be screaming at each other.)* You are not hearin me. He's not comin back here...*ever again.*

RUTHIE ANN. I don't wantta hear you. You've given me another headache. I'm goin back to bed.

MAMA. Go to bed Ruthie Ann. Cover up your head and *pretend* that everthing is all right, cause that's what you been doin for a year. Pretendin that Harry's comin back...pretendin that he loved ya.

RUTHIE ANN. *He did love me!* Now I will not let you take that away from me. He did love me!

MAMA. Harry loved Harry. He was too weak to love anybody else.

RUTHIE ANN. That's not true.

MAMA. You are all you've got and ya best face up to it.

RUTHIE ANN. Stop it Mama. Please just stop it.

MAMA. For twenty years, you gave your life to a lost cause...and you have been defeated. For the love of God...give up!

(At this point there is complete silence.)

RUTHIE ANN. But I had a dream and this dream is what kept me hangin on. I wasn't ready to wake up. Do you understand...I wasn't ready.

MAMA. Even if I did, I wouldn't tell ya so, cause it serves no good purpose.

RUTHIE ANN. I needed time. Him leavin me like that was worse than death. I could get over him dyin and I coulda maybe gotten over this, but I needed time to mourn his passin. I was just tryin to bide me some time.

MAMA. It's been a whole year, Ruthie Ann.

RUTHIE ANN. I know! I know! *(pause)* Ya know I needed him. I needed him so much that you know what I did...I made him weak. I helped him be weak, cause I wanted him that way. *(pause)* He ended up hatin me for it. *(This whole ordeal has completely drained RUTHIE ANN and now that she has been made to admit to herself what she has known all along, she will become a very bitter woman.)* I'll never let myself be hurt like that again. I will never love anybody like that again!

MAMA. I know...and I'm sorry for ya.

RUTHIE ANN. What time did Acia say Milton wanted to see me?

MAMA. He can see ya at 10:30.

RUTHIE ANN. I best go get prepared...I *need* that job.

CURTAIN
End of Scene One - Act Two

SCENE TWO

As the scene opens, it's dark outside and the lamps are on in the house. On the table is a plate of cookies, a jug of wine and several glasses. MAMA is sitting in her easy chair, putting the hem in the dress she's made during the day. SYBIL is eating a cookie and she and RUTHIE ANN are sitting at the table, going over the nominations for Homecoming Queen.

RUTHIE ANN. Sybil, we don't have much choice here. We only got five nominations.

SYBIL. Where's Acia? She's gripin about my bein late and she's late herself.

RUTHIE ANN. *(abruptly)* Didn't see her today. Saw Milton about that job though.

SYBIL. You really gonna work at The Blue Moon?

RUTHIE ANN. Start Saturday night. Mama thinks it's time I live in the real world...can't get much realer than The Blue Moon Cafe. *(MAMA says nothing.)*

SYBIL. Well, I'll be dumbed. Never thought I'd live to see the day Ruthie Ann Castro would walk into a bar, let alone work in one. Just goes to show what I know. *(pause)* Don't ya have anything else to eat? I like chocolate chip cookies, but don't ya ever have anything else?

MAMA. Potato chips in there, if ya want some.

SYBIL. Do potato chips have carbohydrates in'um? *(pause)* What are carbohydrates anyway?

RUTHIE ANN. You're the teacher. You're suppose to know that kinda thing.

SYBIL. I teach little kids. I don't know nothin about science...and Lord how I hate teachin.

MAMA. Ya shoulda never become a teacher then, Sybil. Mamas send their little ones off to school, hopin they'll get some learnin and you're standin up there hatin what you're doin. *(pause)* What kinda warpin ya think that's doin to their little heads?

SYBIL. I'm not tryin to warp nobody's little head. I tell'um one and one is two and let it go at that.

MAMA. Feelin like ya do...you could tell'um one and one is six.

SYBIL. But it's not so Mama Wallace. Math's a science.

MAMA. Said ya don't know nothin about science.

SYBIL. Not science science I don't. *(pause)* I will have some potato chips.

MAMA. *(gets up to get them)* I'll get'um for ya, but are you sure they're on your diet?

SYBIL. *(already convinced herself they are)* Of course. *(MAMA grins to herself and exits to the kitchen.)*

RUTHIE ANN. This is gonna be a awful chore, decidin with just five girls here.

SYBIL. *(referring to the ballots)* Who are the nominees?

RUTHIE ANN. We have Lucy Bates, Alma Roberts, Elizabeth Taylor...ain't it a kick Elizabeth bein named after a movie star?

SYBIL. Since she looks like a horse...shoulda been named Trigger Taylor.

RUTHIE ANN. *(still looking at the ballots)* Jan Carter and Lois Butler.

SYBIL. *Lois Butler!* But she's a whore...we can't have a whore for Homecomin Queen. Who nominated her...-one of her satisfied customers?

RUTHIE ANN. Could be, cause this card's not signed.

SYBIL. Then she'd be ineligible.

RUTHIE ANN. The Committee Rules never said the nomination cards had to be signed.

(MAMA comes back into the room carrying a bag of potato chips. She puts them in front of SYBIL and she begins to eat them.)

SYBIL. Where do all these girls live now?

RUTHIE ANN. Alma, Jan and Lucy live outta state. Last time I talked to Lucy, she said they might come back for the reunion. Her husband's gotta weeks vacation comin.

SYBIL. Who we gonna pick?

RUTHIE ANN. I don't know. Only choice from around here is Elizabeth or Lois.

SYBIL. Not much of a choice...a horse or a whore. *(pause)* Well, what about Alma or Jan?

RUTHIE ANN. They live clean across the country. They won't be back.

MAMA. Pick Lucy Bates and pray to God she shows up. She always was a pleasant person.

RUTHIE ANN. Even Lucy married a idiot.

MAMA. Lotta people marry wrong.

RUTHIE ANN. Well I sure did. But then ya told me so, ain't that right Mama? *(MAMA and RUTHIE ANN look at each other, but MAMA says nothing.)*

SYBIL. *(feeling the tension)* Not me Mama Wallace. I

never got married, so I can't be wrong.

MAMA. Why didn't you get married?

SYBIL. I'm fat, that's why. *(pause)* Can I have some of that wine?

RUTHIE ANN. Yeah, pour ya a big glass. I'm sure it's on your diet. *(SYBIL just looks at her and then pours herself a glass.)*

MAMA. Sybil, there's alotta fat people around who are married.

SYBIL. They got fat *after* they got married. *(pause)* You gotta be skin and bones to catch a man.

MAMA. Hogwash!

SYBIL. It's the truth. Anyway, I've devoted my life to teachin and trainin young minds...the leaders of tomorrow.

MAMA. Hatin teachin like ya do, how you trainin these young minds? You showin'um how to build nuclear bombs or somethin?

SYBIL. *(laughs)* That's science science, Mama Wallace. Only thing I build in my class is indigestion. *(going off into her own little world)* Oh, if only my Mama woulda let me do what I wanted to, I'd be a great ballerina by now. I'd be doin Swan Lake, floatin across a stage on my toes...captivatin a audience with my ability. *(coming out of it and to the others)* Miss Farrell said I was the best dancer she ever taught.

MAMA. I went to your recital when you was in the fifth grade. *(thinking to herself)* You was dressed like some kinda chicken or somethin.

SYBIL. I wasn't a *chicken*...I was a *woodpecker*. We danced to the Woody Woodpecker song. My costume was black and I had pink feathers on my head and tail.

RUTHIE ANN. You can't do a ballet dance to a woodpecker song.

SYBIL. Yes ya can and I was the best woodpecker in the bunch, cause Miss Farrell told me so.

RUTHIE ANN. Yeah I'm sure you were Sybil. A silly song for a sillier idea.

SYBIL. Well, I'm not sayin the song's not silly, but my dance was real good...I always was a good ballet dancer.

MAMA. It was a cute little bit, Ruthie Ann.

RUTHIE ANN. *(sarcastic)* With Sybil involved, I'm sure there was nothin *little* about it. *(SYBIL and MAMA glare at her.)*

(There's a knock at the door and MISS ELLY comes on in.)

ELLY. It's me Mama, comin to check on how your dress is comin along.

MAMA. Have a seat Elly...almost finished hemmin it up. How's your knee feel?

ELLY. Some better, but don't let me use wine for medicine anymore. Forgot to tell ya this mornin, but last night I burned up my fried okra and smoked up my house besides. *(pause)* I'm goin back to anacin or I'm liable to find myself livin in a tent. *(They all laugh, except RUTHIE ANN.)*

SYBIL. Want some potato chips, Miss Elly?

ELLY. Naw, I just ate supper. Had fresh tomatoes... sure were good too.

RUTHIE ANN. Where'd ya get fresh tomatoes this time of year?

ELLY. *(to RUTHIE ANN)* Bought'um offa truck over in Athens, today. *(to MAMA)* Saw Acia there. Was with the same fellow we saw her with on Wednesday...they was huggin and kissin all over the street. She don't even try and hide it anymore.

RUTHIE ANN. If somebody should happen to tell Milton about it, he's just liable to blow her head off. *(MAMA and ELLY look at each other.)*

MAMA. *(to RUTHIE ANN)* You gonna be the one?

SYBIL. *(not knowing what's gone on before)* Nobody rats on ya best friend...ain't that right, Ruthie Ann?

RUTHIE ANN. If you say so, Sybil.

SYBIL. Besides, ya can't judge friends or ya won't have any. Figure Acia's got her reasons for doin what she does. *(pause)* She's not been happy with Milton since the day they got married. Pretty as Acia is, she coulda gone onto Hollywood or somethin...she's smart too, Acia is, coulda left here and been anything she had a mind to, but Milton promised her the moon not to leave him and she got it all right...The Blue Moon Cafe.

ELLY. Guess she felt sorry for him.

RUTHIE ANN. *(Is going to be surprised by some of these revelations, as she's never heard of some of them.)* Sorry for him? Whatever for?

MAMA. He was wounded in action in Korea. Came home a hero really. Why the whole town turned out that day we had the parade for him.

RUTHIE ANN. What parade? I don't remember any parade.

SYBIL. You was off with Harry someplace...you was always off with Harry someplace.

MAMA. There was flags a flyin...bands a playin and confetti all over the place. *(pause)* Yeah, Milton was a real hero that day.

ELLY. That was the day I got drunk on beer. First time I'd ever tasted beer and it was so delicious, I couldn't help myself. I drank and drank and drank...till I was drunk as a skunk.

MAMA. *(laughing remembering)* I had to tuck you in bed that night Miss Elly and we was gigglin and talkin about our husbands. How much fun it'd been to rile'um up and then pout about it till they brought us a present.

ELLY. *(laughing too)* And a real good pout, one like Mount Rushmore, brought us a whole pound of Whitman's Samplers.

SYBIL. Candy! Candy and donuts have been my down fall. *(pause)* Well, Acia got her hero. She's now First Lady of Coleridge...what a honor.

RUTHIE ANN. I never knew Milton was wounded in the war...never seen him limp or nothin.

MAMA. Rumor has it, he got hit where it hurts a *woman* the most...Acia married him anyway. Guess it didn't matter to her.

RUTHIE ANN. You sayin Milton can't...well are you sayin...

MAMA. Not sayin it...it's just rumored, that's all.

ELLY. Coleridge Rumor Factory does turn outta lot of product. Trouble is, can't tell what's good or bad.

RUTHIE ANN. Looks like Acia woulda confided somethin like that to me. I was one of her best friends.

SYBIL. Acia's prideful. She don't cry on nobody's

shoulder. *(pause)* Hard to believe you never heard these things. What'd you do all those years you was married...-bury your head in the sand?

RUTHIE ANN. Never had another thought for nothin, but Harry. He had my attention from mornin till night. Never even had time for my Mama, when Harry was around. *(pause)* Ain't that right, Mama?

MAMA. Never saw ya much.

RUTHIE ANN. *(thinking to herself)* I loved my house. I was happy cleanin from mornin till Harry got there. *(snaps back and to everybody)* Had the cleanest house in Coleridge. You coulda ate off my floors, they was so clean. Use to fuss at Harry all the time, cause he was so sloppy...would just track mud all across my lineoleum and never look back.

MAMA. You shoulda had more outside interest.

RUTHIE ANN. That's right, Mama! You can rest assured I won't be makin that mistake again.

MAMA. *(As she finishes putting the hem in the dress.)* That does it. *(She holds up the dress.)* Turned out real pretty, if I say so myself.

RUTHIE ANN. Glad to see you gotta talent for somethin. Least ways you won't ever have to work in a beer joint.

MAMA. You'll develop a talent, Ruthie Ann.

RUTHIE ANN. Oh, I intend to...a real good talent.

SYBIL. *(referring to MAMA'S dress)* I like pink. Pink always reminds me of my woodpecker costume...is this all the potato chips?

MAMA. Fritos in there, if ya want some.

SYBIL. *(Who has by now already convinced herself that prac-*

tically nothing has carbohydrates in it.) Think I will. Corn's good for ya. We grow corn right here in Freestone County. *(pause)* I'm starved...didn't hardly have any supper, just a head of cauliflower.

ELLY. Sybil, you ate a whole head of cauliflower?

SYBIL. *(as she exits)* A *small* head...why it was hardly enough to keep a bird alive.

MAMA. Wonder what kinda bird she's talkin about... a ostrich.

RUTHIE ANN. Ya'll like to make fun of people, don't ya. *(pause)* Two little ole ladies runnin around together all the time...gigglin and talkin...not *pretendin* at all.

MAMA. That'll be enough Ruthie Ann.

RUTHIE ANN. Acia says Sybil's sick and needs to see a psychiatrist, but I'm figurin she's not the only one around here who's probably sick in the head.

MAMA. Look, I know you're upset about this mornin, but...

RUTHIE ANN. *(interrupts)* Upset! I'm not upset. Why I've got the world by the tail. I'm finally wakin up, ain't that what you wanted? *(pause)* You know Miss Elly, I wantta thank ya for tellin me about Harry and Acia...I owe ya one. Wantta know what Acia thinks about you and Mama?

MAMA. You just better hush your mouth!

RUTHIE ANN. *(continues)* She thinks you're queer, ain't that right Mama?

ELLY. It's not true. We're just good friends, that's all.

MAMA. *(to ELLY)* You don't have to defend our friendship to her. *(pause)* Don't you have a cameo broach?

ELLY. Yeah, one you gave me when we graduated high school.

MAMA. Go get it. I'm thinkin it'll go perfect with this dress. I'll be there in a second.

RUTHIE ANN. *(as ELLY walks out)* Have a nice evenin, Miss Elly.

ELLY. *(turns back to her)* I was plannin on it. *(She looks at her and then MAMA and then exits.)*

MAMA. *(to RUTHIE ANN)* That was uncalled for.

RUTHIE ANN. Why Mama, I was just quotin Acia and you've always admired her haven't ya? Always wanted me to be just like her...pretty and full of fun.

MAMA. That's not so.

RUTHIE ANN. I know where I went wrong. I am gonna be just like her...a husband screwin whore, cause that's a *real woman,* ain't it Mama?

MAMA. I feel sorry for ya, Ruthie Ann.

RUTHIE ANN. Oh don't pity me Ole Lady, cause from now on out, I'm gonna get by in this world *my* way and I will be prepared.

MAMA. Destroy yourself if ya want. I can't help ya anymore.

RUTHIE ANN. Bein a whore hasn't destroyed Acia and you have great compassion for her don't ya? *(MAMA doesn't answer.)* Where was your compassion for me Ole Lady! *(Again MAMA doesn't answer.)* Answer me!

MAMA. I'm answerin nothin!

RUTHIE ANN. Then you better go to your nearest and dearest girlfriend and do whatever ya'll do over there.

MAMA. *(reaches out and slaps her)* I never and I mean never wantta hear you talk about me and Miss Elly like that again. *(They both stare at each other.)*

RUTHIE ANN. Well, I thought as long as we were all bein truthful around here...no need to *pretend* any-more.

MAMA. It's time for you to pack your bags...time for you to move on.

(They both look at each other and MAMA exits out the door and the telephone rings and SYBIL peeps around the kitchen door.)

SYBIL. *(to RUTHIE ANN)* You gonna answer it? *(RUTHIE ANN says nothing.)* Want me to get it? *(Again RUTHIE ANN says nothing and SYBIL comes out of kitchen and goes and picks up the phone.)* Hello. *(pause)* She's not here yet, Milton. *(pause)* Yeah, wait a minute. *(to RUTHIE ANN)* He wants to talk to you.

RUTHIE ANN. *(goes to the phone)* Whatta ya want Milton? *(pause)* I don't have any damned red blouse. *(pause)* Look! I'm comin in Saturday night, but I don't have any red blouse to wear...

(At this time ACIA comes bursting through the door and she is flushed and pretty and is carrying a grocery sack.)

ACIA. *(upon entering)* My friends are we gonna party or are we not.

SYBIL. Acia Darlin...you're late...we been sittin here twiddlin our thumbs waitin on ya. *(getting back at her for yesterday)* Milton's on the phone.

ACIA. *(to RUTHIE ANN)* Tell him I'm not here.

RUTHIE ANN. *(holds out the phone to her)* Tell him yourself!

ACIA. *(Goes and puts the bag of groceries on the table and then goes to the phone.)* Yeah. *(pause)* So, ya found me, that should make ya happy. *(pause)* Wasn't in Athens today, don't know why he'd say that. *(pause)* Shoppin in Birmingham for a dress for Homecomin. *(pause)* I'm not comin out there Milton, till we pick a queen...yell all ya want. *(She slams down the phone and goes to table and digs in the sack. To SYBIL.)* Guess what I got for ya?

SYBIL. What?

ACIA. *(She brings out a six pack of beer and a dozen donuts.)* Feast your eyes on this. Don't that make your saliva glands just stand up and shout.

SYBIL. Beer and donuts! Why those things could be loaded with carbohydrates.

ACIA. They're all creamed filled to be washed down with beer imported all the way from Germany.

SYBIL. *(as though in a trance)* Creamed filled from Germany. *(then back)* You lied to Milton. Miss Elly saw you over in Athens today.

ACIA. *(laughs)* I can't seem to go nowhere Miss Elly don't see me. She's kinda like Spring...always just around the corner. *(Pause and to RUTHIE ANN.)* We need a beer opener here.

RUTHIE ANN. I'll get you one. *(She exits to the kitchen.)*

SYBIL. *(After she exits and almost in a whisper to ACIA.)* I been hidin in the kitchen.

ACIA. What from?

SYBIL. Ruthie Ann and Mama Wallace are fightin.

ACIA. *(As she gets her purse and lights a cigarette.)* What about?

SYBIL. Those rumors regardin her and Miss Elly. You

suppose they're true?

ACIA. Always liked Miss Elly, but I think they are.

SYBIL. I heard'um just yellin and screamin at each other and I was afraid to ask where the fritos were, cause I couldn't find'um.

ACIA. Well, I've made it up to ya with the donuts...and I'm in high spirits tonight and I'll be damned if I'm gonna let anybody dampen'um, either.

(RUTHIE ANN comes back into the room with the beer opener and gives it to ACIA.)

RUTHIE ANN. Here!

ACIA. I'll open'um and we can all drink a toast. *(She takes the beer opener and opens them each a beer and hands it to them.)* Now, here's to my freedom.

SYBIL. What's that mean?

ACIA. And Sybil you gotta eat some of these donuts, but don't ya go eatin all of'um cause custard filled donuts is one of my favorite things in the whole world. *(She hands her a donut.)*

RUTHIE ANN. *(Walks over and picks up the box and shoves it at SYBIL.)* Go ahead and eat the whole box Sybil, so she can call ya a cow to your face.

ACIA. My...my what's the matter with you tonight Ruthie Ann? You wake up on the wrong side of the bed or somethin this mornin?

SYBIL. *(Takes the box and puts it back down and then to RUTHIE ANN.)* I think I will have just one. *(She reaches in and takes one donut and starts to eat it.)* Oh, this is so yummy and I don't think donuts have any carbohydrates. *(pause)*

Sure wish I knew what a carbohydrate was.

RUTHIE ANN. You know what a carbohydrate is Sybil!

SYBIL. *(Caught now in the lies she's been telling herself.)* Well...I think it's somethin found in fish. I never eat any fish.

RUTHIE ANN. *(So bitter about SYBIL's betrayal of her in not telling her of ACIA and HARRY, that she is now going to try and destroy SYBIL'S illusion, just like hers was destroyed.)* Come on, who you tryin to fool. *(pause)* You stuff yourself fat, cause you're afraid of the truth...you're a loser, just like the rest of us, but then you like to act dumb about it, ain't that right?

ACIA. *(eyes RUTHIE ANN)* You not only got out on the wrong side of the bed this mornin, Ruthie Ann...looks to me like ya kinda got out on the cruel side too.

RUTHIE ANN. *(turns on her)* Yeah well, you oughta know about cruelty. *(Grabs a donut and shoves it at SYBIL.)* Here! Stuff yourself like a pig and then pretend you're on a diet. *(SYBIL just looks at her and then hangs her head down and RUTHIE ANN throws the donut on the table.)* By the way Sybil, did you know that my Harry and Acia were a thing at one time?

SYBIL. Ah! Well...I ah...

RUTHIE ANN. *(raises her voice)* Did you know!

ACIA. *(to RUTHIE ANN)* When did you find out?

RUTHIE ANN. Yesterday...I found out yesterday. Mama hit me upside the head with it, sayin she was tryin to wake me up. Was a rude awaknin, that's for sure. *(to SYBIL)* Why didn't you tell me?

SYBIL. *(Has her head practically down on the table.)*

Ah...well, you're my friend and Acia's my friend...didn't figure it was my place.

RUTHIE ANN. Told Mama, told Miss Elly. Told everbody but me, your best friend. *(raises her voice again)* You owed it to me!

ACIA. Yeah well, tell her what a good friend she was Sybil, the whole time she was married to her Harry.

RUTHIE ANN. *(to ACIA)* You just shut up! I'm not talkin to you. *(Pause. To SYBIL.)* Your friend here, calls you a fat cow to your face and you act like you enjoy it and as close as we've been, you owed it to me.

SYBIL. *(Has now had enough and jumps up from the table and to RUTHIE ANN.)* Close! Since when have we been close? Since Harry left that's when, and you had nothin left, but me. So, don't you go tellin me I *owe* you anythin. When you was married to him, I might as well not even been here. Ever time I went over to your house, you were cleanin somethin, wouldn't even stop long enough to talk and when Harry came home...most of the time you never even saw me leave. I just let my ownself out. *(pause)* I owe you nothin!

RUTHIE ANN. *(to ACIA)* Seems like I been wrong all the way around...and you...you the belle of Freestone County, get everthing you want.

ACIA. Not everthing.

RUTHIE ANN. You got my husband it seems.

ACIA. Nothin permanent. I was just a port in his storm.

RUTHIE ANN. And me in my safe little harbor...the good little housewife...bakin cookies...scrubbin floors. Waitin to give him everthing he needed.

ACIA. You were waitin to give him what *you* needed.

RUTHIE ANN. Well...I'm gonna be just like you...give ya some competition. Gonna go out to The Blue Moon, have me some real fun. Screw all the men. Maybe even screw Milton, less of course it was shot off in the war.

SYBIL. Ruthie Ann!

ACIA. *(to RUTHIE ANN)* Now, you'll just have to find that out for yourself...won't ya? Anyway, have at it, cause I could give a rat's ass. *(goes over to SYBIL)* I gotta friend...a real good friend and him and me are leavin this hick town tonight.

SYBIL. Tonight! You can't leave tonight. You gotta give this more thought.

ACIA. Been thinkin and thinkin. *(pause)* There's a whole world waitin out there for me, that I've never even seen. I wantta smoke my cigarettes, wear short shorts when I've a mind and most of all...I need to find me some peace.

SYBIL. But what about Homecomin? Now, we been plannin on Homecomin for six months.

ACIA. Homecomin'll have to wait for me. Nominate me next year Sybil and I'll come back as your queen.

SYBIL. We hadn't picked our queen for this year, yet.

ACIA. Best do it now, cause I gotta meet my friend.

SYBIL. We got no choice this year. It's between a horse, a whore and a long shot of Lucy Bates comin back to Coleridge.

ACIA. I cast my vote for Lois Butler.

SYBIL. Now damn it Acia she's a whore and...

ACIA. Whore or no whore, she gets my vote. I want her

to have a moment of glory, even a whore should have her day.

SYBIL. Well, there's no way we can have a whore for Homecomin Queen...we can just nullify your vote.

RUTHIE ANN. Acia wants a whore for Homecomin Queen and I think we should give it to her. I'm sure she knows what bein a whore is like. I cast my vote for Lois Butler, too.

SYBIL. Now, wait just one minute.

RUTHIE ANN. *(to ACIA)* You're not even regrettin you and Harry are ya?

ACIA. It's in the past, it can't be changed.

RUTHIE ANN. Know you don't care nothin bout the past, but there are people who base their whole futures on it.

ACIA. Then they're fools.

RUTHIE ANN. I trusted you...I trusted Harry and ya'll did that to me.

ACIA. I'll tell you the truth about Harry, Ruthie Ann. He liked to drink...have a good time...kid the girls...

RUTHIE ANN. And you were one of the girls he kidded...*my friend.*

ACIA. Harry found him somebody to laugh with and he's just plain happy now. *(pause)* He don't have to take off his shoes when he comes in the back door, either. *(RUTHIE ANN reaches out and throws beer in her face from a bottle she's drinking out of.)*

ACIA. *(Just looks at her and wipes the beer from her face with the back of her hand.)* He was a lonely drownin man and you were too busy bein the perfect housewife to even see it. *(She walks over to SYBIL.)* I'll write ya when I get settled in some place.

SYBIL. *(hugs her)* You can't leave...you're the First Lady of Coleridge.

ACIA. *(laughs)* You're a real corker, Sybil. I wantta thank ya for makin me laugh all these years. *(She goes and picks up her purse and walks to the door and to RUTHIE ANN.)* Did Milton give ya the job?

RUTHIE ANN. *(with complete hatred)* Oh, I got it all right! Gonna go out to The Blue Moon and be just like you...a port in the storm for the lonely.

ACIA. *(to SYBIL)* Go back on that diet tomorrow ...don't wantta stay a cow all your life. *(She and RUTHIE ANN look at each other and she exits.)*

SYBIL. Can't believe she'd just up and leave like that.

RUTHIE ANN. *(Goes over to the table and pops open another beer and drinks it.)* Wantta beer Sybil. Might make you feel better about her sudden departure.

SYBIL. *(almost to herself)* I love her. Wish I'd told her that. *(She runs to the door and opens it and goes on the porch and then comes back in.)* Damn, she's gone. *(pause)* Maybe you shoulda forgiven her.

RUTHIE ANN. *(laughs)* She didn't ask for my forgiveness. Her bein born pretty and full of fun, she just thinks everthing is her due. Even adultry, with her best friends husband.

SYBIL. I'm not excusin her Ruthie Ann, cause I know how ya loved Harry, but Acia never thinks about what she's doin...she just does it. It's just the way she is and ya can't go tryin' to change people, cause if ya do, they just end up hatin ya for it.

RUTHIE ANN. Not thinkin, that's an excuse in itself, ain't it? *(pause)* Well, I finally know where I messed up. Gonna go out to The Blue Moon...drink like a fish...

SYBIL. You won't be hurtin nobody but yourself.

RUTHIE ANN. Flirt with his honor, the mayor...look at his ole war wounds.

SYBIL. Won't be gettin back at Acia none, cause Milton's a real jerk. She coulda done better than him livin in the Fiji Islands. That's a place I teach about at school...run around there naked...*savages,* is what they are.

RUTHIE ANN. You know Sybil, after all's said and done, neither one of you were really my friends and I could give a *rat's ass (ACIA'S favorite expression and she hits it hard.)* if I ever lay eyes on either one of ya again!

SYBIL. *(just stands there a moment)* Well...I guess I better go then.

RUTHIE ANN. Yeah, why don't ya do just that. *(She walks over to the table and picks up the box of donuts and holds them out to her.)* Take these donuts with ya. Stuff yourself with'um tonight and in the mornin *pretend* you coulda been a great ballerina.

SYBIL. *(Gets her purse and books and goes to the door and then back to RUTHIE ANN.)* Thank ya for your honesty, Ruthie Ann. I'm sure you'll be rewarded for it someday. *(pause)* I got class in the mornin...Lord, how I hate teachin. I'm gonna hit those little bastards up with a terrible test first thing. *(She exits out the door.)*

(RUTHIE ANN starts to clean off the table and exits to the kitchen, she then comes back into the room and opens another beer

and goes to the window and looks out. Enter MAMA, still holding her dress that she exited with. When she enters RUTHIE ANN turns and faces her.)

RUTHIE ANN. Hope you enjoy wearin your pretty pink dress for Homecomin, cause it'll be to honor a whore. *(pause)* Lois Butler! And Homecomin Queen she's gonna be. Won't her Mama be beamin.
MAMA. You confront Acia about Harry?
RUTHIE ANN. Oh, I talked to her all right and you was right, she knew Harry better than I ever did. *(pause)* Now, that she's gone, you're lookin at the next first Lady of Coleridge.
MAMA. Gone?
RUTHIE ANN. Yeah, she just roped herself a sucker and took off.
MAMA. Where?
RUTHIE ANN. How the shit should I know.

(The telephone rings.)

RUTHIE ANN. That'll be Milton, wonderin where his honey is...he's a bigger fool than me. *(pause)* What should I tell him Mama, that his honey is a whore. What would you do, if you were me?
MAMA. Do what you have to.

(RUTHIE ANN goes to the telephone as it still rings and places her hand on the phone, but doesn't pick it up.)

RUTHIE ANN. Whores don't rat on whores. They just

try and take over their territory. *(The phone stops ringing and RUTHIE ANN picks up her beer and goes to the window and MAMA is still standing in the middle of the room. RUTHIE ANN looks out into the front yard.)* Tomorrow, I'm gonna unpack all those ole trophies and throw'um in the trash. Then, I'm gonna go out and buy myself a red blouse, cause I look good in red. *(pause)* Come see the moonlight shinin on your wisteria bush. *(As she leans up against the window sill and takes a big swig of beer.)* It's not gonna blossom for you, come next Spring. *(She turns to her mother.)* No flowers for Mama...not a single one.

(They both continue to look at each other and the lights fade. Curtain!.)

COSTUME PLOT

ACT ONE

RUTHIE ANN — dark colored slacks, drab colored blouse, low-heeled dark colored shoes

MAMA WALLACE — gingham house dress, glasses, old shoes, with socks

ACIA — tight fitting designer jeans, very tight fitting tee-shirt, high heel shoes, a purse

MISS ELLY — house dress, old shoes, cane

SYBIL — large sacky looking dress, sweater, low-heeled shoes

ACT TWO — SCENE ONE

MAMA WALLACE — robe, house shoes, glasses

MISS ELLY — baggy slacks, loose fitting blouse, floppy hat

RUTHIE ANN — robe, house shoes

ACT TWO — SCENE TWO

RUTHIE ANN — different colored dark slacks, blouse

SYBIL — bright colored sacky dress

MAMA WALLACE — house dress of a different pattern,
    shoes, socks, glasses

MISS ELLY — house dress, cane, low-heeled shoes

ACIA — attractive tight fitting dress, high heel shoes,
    purse

PROPERTY PLOT

ACT ONE

1. family pictures in frames on coffee table
2. old fashioned lace or sheer curtains at window
3. crocheted doilies in a variety of patterns and colors on arms of couch, chairs and on tables
4. old coffee cups on dining table
5. telephone on telephone table
6. gardening book on bookshelf
7. sugar bowl and creamer (Ruthie Ann)
8. cigarette out of purse (Acia)
9. ashtray, behind books in bookcase
10. coffee pot (Mama Wallace)
11. saccharin (Ruthie Ann)
12. pink cotton material (Mama Wallace)
13. dress pattern (Mama Wallace)
14. nomination forms for Homecoming Queen in bookcase (Ruthie Ann)
15. two glasses, bottle of wine (Acia)
16. scissors, pin cushion (Mama Wallace)
17. cane (Miss Elly)
18. broom and dustpan (Acia)
19. glass (Mama Wallace)
20. wash cloth (Ruthie Ann)
21. gallon bottle of wine (Acia)
22. glass (Acia)
23. books and paper sack (Sybil)
24. shovel (Mama Wallace)
25. wash cloth (Ruthie Ann)

ACT TWO — SCENE ONE

1. coffee pot on dining table
2. coffee cups on sideboard
3. gardening book in bookcase

ACT TWO — SCENE TWO

1. plate of cookies on dining table
2. jug of wine on dining table
3. several glasses on dining table
4. nomination forms for Homecoming Queen on dining table
5. pink dress (Mama Wallace holding)
6. potato chips (Mama Wallace)
7. grocery sack (Acia)
8. six-pack imported beer
9. dozen donuts
10. beer opener (Ruthie Ann)
11. pink dress (Mama Wallace)